Oral History and Business

This book introduces business historians to oral history methodologies and approaches.

Using four distinct oral history case studies to explore ideas of disruption and continuity in business history over the second half of the twentieth century, Robert Crawford and Matthew Bailey demonstrate how critical engagement with oral history approaches serves to enhance and enliven business history as well as its relationship with other historical fields. The focus on disruption is used to encompass a broad set of processes such as technological change, the impact of external forces, informal business networks, social constructions of gender, knowledge transfer, firm adaptability and cultural change. The use of oral histories to interpret responses to disruption in the past, and to explore the features characterising business continuity, provides an opportunity to consider the human dimensions, subjective experiences and personal insights of workplace, firm and industry change. It also sheds light on the ways that people and firms respond to disruptive forces through innovation and adaptation – both successfully and unsuccessfully.

This succinct and accessible account is essential reading for business historians with little experience in using oral history, as well as those looking to gain deeper insights from their oral history data.

Robert Crawford is a Professor of Advertising in the School of Media and Communication at RMIT University. His research focuses on the growth and development of the advertising, marketing and public relations industries. His recent books include *More than a Glass and a Half: A History of Cadbury in Australia* (Halstead, 2022), *Digital Dawn in Adland: Transforming Australian Agencies* (Routledge, 2021) and *Decoding Coca-Cola: A Biography of a Global Brand* (Routledge, 2021, co-edited with Linda Brennan and Susie Khamis).

Matthew Bailey is a Senior Lecturer in the Department of History and Archaeology at Macquarie University. He is one of Australia's leading retail historians. His book, *Managing the Marketplace: Reinventing Shopping Centres in Post-War Australia* (Routledge, 2020), is the first book on the subject, and one of the few to comprehensively examine Australian retail history. He has published widely on retail and retail property history, including in leading international and Australian journals such as *Urban History, Journal of Urban History, Enterprise & Society* and *Australian Economic History Review.* He is currently working on an ARC-funded project on the history of department stores.

Oral History and Business
Disruption and Continuity

Robert Crawford
Matthew Bailey

Routledge
Taylor & Francis Group

LONDON AND NEW YORK

First published 2023
by Routledge
4 Park Square, Milton Park, Abingdon, Oxon OX14 4RN

and by Routledge
605 Third Avenue, New York, NY 10158

Routledge is an imprint of the Taylor & Francis Group, an informa business

© 2023 Robert Crawford and Matthew Bailey

British Library Cataloguing-in-Publication Data
A catalogue record for this book is available from the British Library

Library of Congress Cataloging-in-Publication Data
A catalog record has been requested for this book

ISBN: 978-0-367-77406-6 (hbk)
ISBN: 978-0-367-77405-9 (pbk)
ISBN: 978-1-003-17123-2 (ebk)

DOI: 10.4324/9781003171232

Typeset in Times New Roman
by codeMantra

Contents

Acknowledgements   vii

Introduction: A Disrupted Conversation   1

1 Managing Disruption: Business Change,
  Organisational Politics, and Work Life Balance   24

2 Creating Continuity: Stakeholders, Narratives,
  and the Cadbury Brand   45

3 Spatial Continuity: Retail 'Town Halls' in
  Post-War Australia   66

4 Digital Disruption: The Advertising Industry's
  Uneasy Revolution   87

  Conclusion: Continuing the Conversation   110

Index   117

Acknowledgements

While this book reflects our passion for business history and oral history, it also reflects the support and generosity that we have been fortunate to receive.

We would first like to thank the people who have generously agreed to be interviewed for our projects. Spatial restrictions have meant that we could only cite a small percentage of them in this book, but every interviewee who has shared their stories, insights and experiences has directly contributed to this book.

We also acknowledge the support for the project that we have received from the Australian Research Council's Discovery Project scheme (DP220100943).

Our Introduction contains a reworked and updated version of our article 'Cousins once removed? Revisiting the Relationship between Oral History and Business History', which originally appeared in *Enterprise & Society* 20, no. 1 (2019): 4–19. We would like to thank Cambridge University Press and, in particular, Andrew Popp, who encouraged us to produce a themed section on oral history and business history. We would like to thank Mondelēz Australia for access to their Heritage Collection and the State Library of Victoria for access to the Coles Myer archive.

Thank you to Dr Jackie Dickenson for her assistance in bringing this project together and for her insightful feedback on earlier versions of this text.

And finally, we would like to express our deepest thanks for the loving support of our families.

Introduction
A Disrupted Conversation

When visitors seek to download one of the oral history interviews from the National Library of Australia (NLA) catalogue, they are met with the following statement: 'This is important: You are seeking access to an oral history recording. Oral history is by its nature spoken memory. It is a personal opinion and is not intended to present the final verified or complete narrative of events'. While the statement is accurate, it is curious that other items in the NLA's collection do not bear a similar warning. The implication is that oral history needs to be approached with caution – it is unclear whether this is negative or positive. In this book, we argue the latter with the aim of demonstrating how oral history interviews and methodologies can enhance and enrich business history.

Asher Joel's 1973 interview with the oral historian Hazel de Berg is held in the NLA's oral history catalogue. As one of the pioneers of the public relations industry in Australia, it might well be argued that the NLA's cautionary warning is appropriate in this instance. Joel's interview nevertheless offers an opportunity to reflect on the relationship between oral history and business history. However, historians looking for a detailed account of the early days of public relations in Australia might be somewhat underwhelmed by the general nature of Joel's reminiscences. There is little here about disruption or innovation. Explaining that his decision to venture into the business of public relations was born of necessity, Joel pragmatically recounted the difficulties he encountered when returning to civilian life after serving in the Second World War:

> I was on my own again without a job, without any help. And, er, knocking on doors of once prominent people, who were very sympathetic but did nothing about re-establishing or rehabilitating me. But then again, I was able to convince the Australian

DOI: 10.4324/9781003171232-1

government ... that I deserved the allowance, which was being given to help ex-servicemen, particularly those who didn't have any academic training. And I think I got £250, which with my deferred pay enabled me to start a small office in O'Connell Street, Sydney, where I set myself up as a public relations consultant. The first public relations consultant, I think, in Australia.[1]

He also recalled that his decision to set up his public relations consultancy was equally informed by his wartime experiences:

I only found out what public relations meant because I was on [General Douglas] MacArthur's advanced echelon public relations staff and I saw the tremendous power, which was used by MacArthur to mould public opinion, to convey to the world his thoughts in his communiques and the way in which the propaganda of this mighty nation could be used to help the war effort. And I decided that this was a field, somehow or rather, as a result of my journalistic training, I could perhaps become fairly successful in. Well, between now and between then a great deal has happened ...[2]

The interview offers little more insight into or reflections on the challenges or everyday business of running a public relations consultancy – Joel's emphasis on the 'great deal [that] has happened' largely centred on famous names he had met and the big campaigns he had worked on. Joel's interview reminds us that interviews do not always tell us what we expect to hear or even what we want to hear. As such, they demand us to pay close attention and to critically evaluate all aspects of them.

A closer listening of Joel's interview consequently delivers several unforeseen insights into the subject himself, public relations, and the interview process more generally. Joel's narrative, for example, positions him as a dynamic and independent actor, a disruptor who is constructive. He is well connected but makes his own luck. His wartime service demonstrates that he is a man of integrity and discipline, while his experience with MacArthur positions him as experienced and worldly. Joel's outline of the American's use of public relations for the national good seeks to ameliorate suspicions about it and its impact, and to legitimise the presence of public relations in contemporary life. Viewed from this perspective, oral history interviews can be considered performances, where the construction and presentation of interviewee narratives can be as revealing as the details and events recounted in them. As such, oral history presents a particularly rich resource for business historians exploring undocumented or under-documented aspects of business practice – from experiences at the individual level to broader concepts or themes affecting all businesses, such as innovation and disruption.

Business History and Disruption

Disruption is big business. A 2017 article in *The Economist* declared that 'The notion of disruption, with its promise to destroy the status quo and then renew it, is the most fashionable idea in global business since the craze for emerging markets over a decade ago'.[3] Written under the pseudonym 'Schumpeter', the article went on to note that the idea of disruption can sometimes be more powerful than the actual experience of it. Incumbent firms also frequently turn out to be more resilient to change than expected, by absorbing or adapting to disruptive forces that initially appear likely to swamp them. *The Economist*'s 'Schumpeter' column was in fact penned by political editor Adrian Woolridge and touched on ideas he expounded in depth in his 2015 book *The Great Disruption: How Business is Coping with Turbulent Times*. There, Woolridge declared that:

> If the post-war era was the age of Keynes, the modern era is the age of Schumpeter. Entrepreneurs have taken central stage. Change has speeded up. Disruption has become endemic. Over the past two decades there have been innumerable disruptions in almost every industry under the sun, disruptions that have not only forced incumbents to fight for their life but have frequently turned assets into liabilities and business models into prisons. So many disruptions, in fact, that they add up to one great disruption: a great disruption not of 'traditional society' of the sort Marx chronicled but of capitalism itself.[4]

While the internet has certainly revolutionised capitalist markets, business operations, and the nature of consumption, the magnitude of such change should not mask the profound upheavals and innovations of other times. The post-war years may well have been 'the age of Keynes' when the welfare state provided a bedrock of economic stability, but managers, employees and consumers also experienced waves of disruption that fundamentally transformed business, work and everyday life.

As Woolridge notes, Joseph Schumpeter provides highly useful insights into these processes. For Schumpeter, innovation was a pre-requisite for pursuing business profits: businesses are incentivised to innovate by the difference in profit produced by undertaking research and development compared with not doing so.[5] In identifying and articulating the key role of innovation, Schumpeter was influential in developing the idea of capitalism as an adaptive system.[6] This was in contrast to most of his peers, who viewed innovation as an exogenous economic factor.[7] For Schumpeter, innovation was intrinsic to economics and came in a variety of forms: the introduction of new products or new qualities in existing products; the opening up of new markets; the creation of new industry structures; the development of new production methods and transportation technologies; and the creation of new sources of supply. Entrepreneurs and businesses introducing such innovations fuelled 'the capitalist engine'[8] by introducing the 'competition that matters'.[9] That is, the new ways of doing things or new goods or services that rendered obsolete the status quo. Schumpeter declared that capitalism was, thus, 'by nature a form or method of economic change … a process of industrial mutation that incessantly revolutionizes the economic structure *from within*, incessantly destroying the old one, incessantly creating a new one'. Labelling this process 'creative destruction', Schumpeter considers it to be 'the essential fact about capitalism'.[10]

One consequence of this gale of creative destruction is that those firms that fail to adequately innovate or to respond to the innovations of competitors will lose their market share and may even face closure or takeover. Correspondingly, those businesses that successfully innovate succeed, or, at least, remain viable enterprises.[11] Creative destruction, then, does not necessarily destroy incumbent firms. Disruptive innovation is frequently, and perhaps a little romantically, attached to founders of innovative startups, or 'Schumpeterian entrepreneurs'. However, as Schumpeter himself observed, there are considerable incentives for established firms to innovate. As Chapter 1 shows, this occurred in Australian retailing when the country's largest firms chose to introduce retail formats that took market share from their existing chains rather than risk a rival firm doing the same. In such cases, established firms can drive the evolution of industries and lead forays into new markets.[12] Subsequently, parallel to stories of decline and loss, creative destruction also provides a lens to observe how different firms manage and adapt to change, maintain continuity, and seize opportunities to grow in disrupted marketplaces. Even within those firms and industries that maintain or grow their market share, forms of destruction (or loss) are evident as innovation pushes aside established practices. This, Schumpeter believed, was the 'necessary complement' of development.

In contrast to his econometric peers who pursued mechanistic explanations of innovation based on mathematical models, Schumpeter presented organic analogies to explain the evolution of capitalism. Writing to the econometrist and later Nobel Prize winner, Ragnar Frisch, in 1931, Schumpeter argued that:

> there is an agent, within the economic world which alters data and with these the economic process: entrepreneurial activity, which I [consider] ... as something *sui generis* ... It not only destroys existing equilibrium, but also that circuit-like process of economic life, it makes economic things change instead of making them recur ... Biological mutations [are the best] analogy.[13]

Although Schumpeter received criticism for his refusal to provide formal models (particularly as he sought to unpack the nature of innovation in later works), his organic approach offers a useful framework for business historians today who are increasingly attracted to the social and cultural dimensions of business change.[14] For Schumpeter, the driver of such change was a subject, the entrepreneur, whose act of innovation was, by definition, a deviation from the norm, a subjective and individual departure from the status quo.[15] Jean-Marie Dru later made a similar point about disruption more generally in his populist business writings, arguing that it 'is about uncovering the culturally embedded biases and conventions that shape standard approaches to business thinking'.[16] While Schumpeter's peers and colleagues challenged him to produce empirical evidence, mathematical formulas, and data to support his claims, we offer a very different form of engagement with his ideas. Instead of producing hard empirical data, we embrace the insight that innovation, entrepreneurial activity, firm capabilities, knowledge transfer and strategic decision-making involve individuals, social networks and informal processes. As Everett M. Rogers notes, the diffusion of innovations is more a social process than it is a technical matter.[17] Moreover, industry and social change are correlated, as evidenced when new technologies infuse products or systems that, in turn, change behaviours.[18]

The other side of Schumpeter's equation, the destruction of existing technologies and practices, also has cultural and social implications, including how employees and managers understand and experience workplace change. As he argued, the mutation of firms or industries via innovations aimed at enhancing profits is inevitably accompanied by the disappearance of some 'businesses, individual positions, forms of life, cultural values and ideals'.[19] Arguing that 'the Schumpeterians have all along gloried in capitalism's endless creativity while treating the destructiveness as mostly a matter of the normal costs of doing business', the Marxist scholar David Harvey suggests that the process of destruction might also offer new insights.[20] The story of destruction flowing from innovation is well covered in scholarship on de-industrialisation, which has explored the enormous job casualties and social implications involved in the transformation of manufacturing industries that had been the foundation for economic growth across the twentieth century.[21] There is, however, more to explore in other industries, not least because the innovation/destruction dynamic is also diffuse, quotidian and, at times, normalised into invisibility. This is the Schumpeterian 'gale'; in places, change is dramatic and spectacular; elsewhere it can be mundane, technical, and incremental. But it is pervasive and endemic to capitalism and its enterprises.[22] Micro-histories of particular firms and industries can thus be revealing of broader national developments or even the evolution of capitalism itself. There is now a considerable literature on the dynamics, differentiating factors, role of external institutions and public actors, and place of sectoral systems involved in these connections.[23] However, considerable work remains to be done to better understand the dynamics of disruption and innovation, its variability across industries and geographic contexts, as well as the generative and mediating roles of actors and institutions.[24]

In his article 'Innovation and the Evolution of Industries', the economist Franco Malerba contends that:

> During its evolution, an industry undergoes a process of transformation that involves knowledge, technologies, learning, the features and competences of actors, types of products and processes, and institutions. An industry also changes its structure, where the term "structure" here means not market structure, but rather the network of relationships (competitive and cooperative, market and non-market, formal and informal) among actors that affect innovation and performance in an industry.[25]

This book seeks to better understand these structures and to add a fresh chapter to extant scholarship by deploying oral history to explore creative destruction. We argue that oral history is particularly valuable for considering the social and cultural implications of both disruption and continuity as well as actors' experiences of these processes.

Business History and Oral History

Oral history and business history share a somewhat checkered past. In the most recent edition of *The Voice of the Past*, Paul Thompson observes that 'the role of oral evidence in economic history has normally been relatively modest', before outlining how business history has benefitted from oral history approaches.[26] However, he only briefly comments on the impact of business history on oral history, suggesting that the contribution largely flows in one direction. Organisers of the 2013 Oral History Society annual conference challenged this standpoint. With the theme 'Corporate Voices: Institutional and Organisational Oral Histories', they asked, 'What can interviews with those who work in businesses, institutions and organisations tell us about organisational history and memory?'.[27] But is this all they offer? In his article 'Corporations are People Too', Rob Perks observes that

> Organisations are made up of people, each with their own personal biographies; but each organisation also has its own "biography," shaped both by its own people's biographies and by the versions of itself that it creates for different purposes at different times.[28]

Perks goes on to claim that 'Oral history is uniquely well-placed to explore these complex relationships between the personal, the public and the corporate'.[29] And, we might add, their broader cultural, social, economic, and political contexts. The opportunities that can be derived from greater engagement between oral historians and business historians have prompted us to write this book. Although a growing number of business historians have begun to pay more serious attention to oral history methodologies, the relationship between the two fields remains largely under-examined and therefore misunderstood.[30]

Business history's absence from oral history can primarily be attributed to the latter's social goal of prioritising the voice of the lay person and its 'entrenched suspicion of big business'.[31] There is also an assumption that business historians have not meaningfully contributed to the development of oral history. This view infers that the evolution of the use and conceptualisation of oral history among business historians is unremarkable and merely follows in the wake of oral historians. However, a closer examination of business history journals challenges this interpretation.

Although the use and discussion of oral history within business history publications correlate with oral history's broader trajectory, the historical lack of engagement between historians working in these fields is significant. By reviewing the use and interpretation of oral history within key business history journals and comparing them with those taking place among oral history more generally, it can be argued that oral history's development within business history has largely operated as a separate strand – albeit one that has recently established more direct connections with broader oral history methodologies and debates. As such, this dialogue between business history and oral history has much to contribute to both fields.

Supplementing the Record

Interviewing eyewitnesses of history has been a research methodology since ancient times and was a key evidentiary component of history writing until the nineteenth century.[32] Even at this point, oral sources remained a valued form of evidence, from Henry Mayhew's surveys of urban working-class life to Jules Michelet's gathering of 'living documents' for his monumental *History of the French Revolution*. Michelet used oral evidence to counterbalance the singular political angle of official documents. 'My inquiry', he wrote, 'among living documents taught me many things that are not in our statistics'.[33]

History's emergence as a professional, academic occupation eroded the value placed on oral testimony. Historical training, which in nineteenth-century Europe was strongly influenced by the empirical approach advocated by Leopold von Ranke, now insisted on the pursuit of facts obtained from documents. Trainee scholars were evaluated on their capacity to produce original work using evidence from primary documents. Documentary research thus gave the profession its own distinct methodology, assessable by its own experts, and a claim to objective neutrality. Von Ranke's approach spread incrementally and inconsistently, from Germany across Europe and to the United States from the 1860s onwards.[34] In contrast to documentary materials, oral evidence was characterised as unreliable and subjective. The use of interviews, however, continued in other fields, notably by private researchers in the nineteenth century as well as Chicago School sociologists. It was not until after the Second World War that the term 'oral history' began being applied to interviews focused on past events and practices.[35]

Business history occupies an important place at the beginning of this modern oral history movement. In 1948, Allan Nevins introduced the pioneering oral history project at Columbia University, where he collated recorded interviews with American elites.[36] The interviews formed the cornerstone of the Columbia archive, which has become one of the largest oral history collections in the world.[37] Nevins's project fulfilled a call by the British economic historian J. H. Clapham some 40 years earlier. Noting the difficulty of accurately interpreting documentary sources on Britain's wool and worsted industries, Clapham claimed that 'the best original authorities are the memories of business-men' and argued for the need to capture them, 'for with [these men] often die some of the most valuable records of nineteenth century economic history'.[38]

Nevins's 'great man' approach defined oral history in the United States for two decades. In contrast, British oral history in the 1950s and 1960s was largely concerned with history from below, giving voice to 'ordinary' people who had been absent from documentary evidence.[39] Despite their differences, the British and American approaches nevertheless concurred that interviews offered important evidence that could be gathered and added to the archive. This book suggests that both perspectives offer a rich vein for business historians.

The use of oral history sources in business history journals has largely followed the methods of the first wave of oral historians. Interviewees were identified as a way of filling gaps in extant documentary records. While their evidence was certainly weighed carefully, it appears to have been analysed as various forms of eyewitness accounts: descriptions of events beyond the direct reach of the historian that helped explain how and why things happened as and when they did. This included insights into the strategies of firms, the reasons for management decision-making, and details of inter-firm transactions.[40] Oral history also gave access to workers' perspectives on particular management strategies as well as their impact on work.[41] It provided evidence about organisational culture shaping ideas and approaches to research and training, and the mechanisms facilitating interaction between firms and business schools.[42] Interviews revealed kinship networks within family firms, and their impact on business decision-making processes.[43] They were used to explore intergenerational change in work-life experience,[44] clashes between personalities and strategies that negatively affected organisational culture,[45] managerial attitudes towards structural change,[46] the reasons and rationale for firms' policy and practice,[47] and the influence of religious affiliation and personal connections on recruitment practices and employment prospects.[48] Oral history proved particularly adept at revealing undocumented details of relationships, including those between government and business,[49] along supply chains,[50] and between executives within firms.[51] It also provided an opportunity to examine mistakes and failed strategies, including the problems arising from joint ventures between firms with different goals and operational practices.[52] Such examples illustrate the wide range of work in business history that utilised oral history to trace otherwise undocumented historical events, practices, beliefs and ideas.

The accounts listed above largely used small numbers of interviews to supplement archival and other documentary sources. This reflects the tenor of the discipline as much as the nature of research projects. But even where considerable use was made of interviews, there was often little critical engagement with the interview process, and few reflections on memory. Business oral history thus shares methodological similarities with early post-war oral history in that the interview was primarily a source of information about factual events.[53] There are, of course, many differences, notably business history's greater engagement with archival, documentary and data sources, and, until at least the mid-1990s, its focus on elites.

Oral historians' uncritical use of interviews during the early post-war period left them open to criticism. Memory, critics noted, 'was distorted by physical deterioration and nostalgia in old age, by the personal bias of both interviewer and interviewee, and by the influence of collective and retrospective versions of the past'.[54] Critics argued that evidence based on memory provided a flimsy base for any substantive argument. Oral historians subsequently sought to construct oral history as a rigorous, scientific methodology.[55] In doing so, they sought to limit the extent to which memory, subjectivity and power relations between interviewer and interviewee distorted qualitative data as it was being gathered.[56]

The formation of the Oral History Association (OHA) in 1967 signalled an important shift. Despite the increased use of oral history interviews during the 1960s, there were no clearly defined parameters, objectives or processes for their recording and interpretation. The OHA sought to professionalise the field by prescribing set forms of practice and technique. The aim was to provide oral histories some authoritative equivalence with the archive.[57] Concerns about methodologies that could produce objective recollections were also a response to positivist thinking, and the difficulties oral historians faced in meeting its exacting standards.[58] In a further counterbalance to this, oral historians also challenged documentary historians about the selectivity and bias inherent in their own sources of evidence.

It was not until the mid-1990s that business history journals contained detailed descriptions of oral history methodologies. A decade later, commentary on data-gathering methods had become more regular, reflecting the field's engagement with broader social science methodological approaches. More recently, such comments have become quite commonplace. Articles usually outline sample sizes, recruitment and interview processes, and reflections on oral history's benefits.[59] The limitations and weaknesses of oral history interviewing have similarly received greater attention.[60] Some researchers have also developed methodological frameworks to counter the approach's limitations.[61]

While such scholarship points to an increased engagement with methodological issues, serious reflection on oral history methodology and interpretation is not yet commonplace. This absence supports calls for business historians to pay greater attention to methodology.[62] It also indicates that despite business history's pioneering contribution to the field of oral history, it has followed its own evolutionary trajectory. A reconnection of these separate strands has occurred in more recent times as a result of intellectual innovations in oral history scholarship entering business history literature.

Recalibrating Oral History

In the late 1970s, and in the face of continuing criticism about memory's subjectivity and fallibility, innovative oral historians turned a weakness into a strength. They claimed that individual subjectivity provided clues about the meaning of history as well as about relationships between memory and identity, and between individuals and society. Memory thus 'became the subject as well as the source of oral history, and oral historians began to use an ... array of approaches – linguistic, narrative, cultural, psychoanalytic and ethnographic – in their analysis and use of oral history interviews'.[63] In the process of implementing these 'new' approaches, business historians have ventured beyond descriptive accounts of oral history practices and cursory nods to its inherent strengths and weaknesses. Over the last decade, business historians have increasingly engaged with broader oral history issues.[64]

Significantly, the growing engagement with oral history has encouraged business historians to engage with other historians utilising and exploring oral history – within business history and beyond. Observing that 'Oral history is a relative newcomer in the accounting history field and has scarcely begun in the management history field', Lee Parker acknowledges oral history's growing presence at the turn of the century but does not comment on the nature of accounting historians' engagement with oral history.[65] In their 1991 assessment of oral history in accounting, Marilyn Collins and Robert Bloom advocated its use 'to confirm or refute any hypotheses involved in analyzing recorded history'.[66] However, they cautioned that it should be used 'to complement the written record, or substitute for the written word if none is available' and included the proviso that 'all researchers using the oral history method should be aware of its limitations'.[67] Challenging this 'functional' stance, Theresa Hammond and Prem Sikka drew on emerging critical scholarship across the academy and within accounting history, as well as oral history historiography to argue that oral history 'should be used to problematize claims that there is a single true universal story to be uncovered and should emphasise the multiplicity of experience that results from accounting practices'.[68] Oral history's placement of everyday human agency into accounting history, they argued, enabled accounting historians to move beyond the standard accounts of regulatory development, professional recognition, and significant personalities. Their call did not fall on deaf ears – accounting historians have since embraced oral history as a tool and methodology with varying degrees of criticality.[69] Significantly, Hammond and Sikka's call has also gained traction in other business fields.[70]

Marketing historians have been receptive to oral history with interviews used as a key resource in several national studies.[71] In his study of Australian advertising executives in Southeast Asia, Robert Crawford has shown that inserting personal experience into business history via oral history can help us understand 'the transmission of business cultures'.[72] Drawing on oral history's radical tradition, other marketing historians have used oral history to move 'beyond an otherwise general reliance on the findings of a small number of contemporaneous market research reports' to develop greater historical understandings of consumers.[73] In revealing the 'consumers' point of view',[74] oral history offers access to 'the meaning ordinary people have given to brands'[75] as well as the 'inner feelings and states of mind that are frequently absent from or disguised by written records'.[76] In her exploration of oral history's contribution to marketing history, Andrea Davies offers further reasons for marketing's receptiveness to oral history. Noting that 'Marketing history also holds the potential to bring a critical understanding of the interview, a ubiquitous method in marketing', Davies not only underscores the discipline's familiarity with interview techniques, she also recognises oral history's capacity to inform contemporary practice.[77]

Management historians have been relatively late converts to oral history. Ronald Mitchell's 1996 analysis of entrepreneurs was one of the first studies to identify itself as an oral history. Significantly, it draws on cognitive information processing theory but makes no reference to oral history scholarship.[78] In their special edition on historical methods for *Management & Organizational History*, Anna Linda Musacchio Adorisio and Alistair Mutch explain Mitchell's approach. Observing the 'considerable sophistication' of debates within oral history historiography around the reliability of memory and its interpretation, Musacchio Adorisio and Mutch contend that similar discussions are to be found in the social sciences. Such differences are thus 'largely illusory, the product more of disciplinary conventions'.[79] Martyna Sliwa's contribution to that collection[80] (and elsewhere)[81] nevertheless indicates that the embrace of oral history among management historians remains limited. Observing the ongoing lack of 'conceptual and empirical exchange between management and organization scholars ... and oral historians', Sliwa ardently urges management and organizational historians to embrace oral history as a tool and a methodology that, she writes, 'changed me as a researcher and as a person'.[82] Over the last decade, management historians have increasingly employed oral history as a tool,[83] and engaged with methodological issues, notably those pertaining to memory.[84] In recent years, oral history's 'method and its disciplinary engagement with memory studies' has become recognised as an 'acceptable' and familiar approach for organisation and work studies scholars[85]; however, an abiding scepticism and a lack of nuanced understanding of it remain.[86]

Within the conventional business history field, researchers demonstrate a growing awareness of methodological debates surrounding oral history. Many papers tread the well-worn path in highlighting oral history's capacity to complement official sources. However, their critical reflections on oral history methodology display greater nuance, drawing on broader debates to recognise the insights afforded by engaging with the complexities of interview data.[87] Geoffrey Jones and Rachael Comunale note that oral histories can reveal why events did *not* occur, expose issues such as corruption, and provide information about business in countries where there exists no strong tradition of archival record keeping.[88] For example, oral histories proved invaluable to Valeria Giacomin, Geoffrey Jones and Eric Salvaj in their study of business investments in education in emerging markets.[89] Noting that 'oral history shows how elements of the linguistic turn can be incorporated, while at the same time remaining understandable by not forgetting to connect history to reality', Ronald Kroeze and Sjoerd Keulen underscore broadening engagements such as these, while reiterating oral history's appropriateness for business historians.[90]

Significantly, the growth of critical awareness across these accounts has also seen business historians interrogate their own contribution to oral history. John Walton thus challenges the view that business historians have been pioneering oral historians and advocates active engagement with oral history debates.[91]

Of course, business historians still have much to do in this space. Despite the growing interaction with broader historical methodologies, various issues remain under-examined. While Patrick Fridenson notes that feminist approaches have 'completely changed our understanding of internal and external labor markets',[92] Gabrielle Durepos, Alan McKinlay and Scott Taylor observe that women in business history 'remain marginal to central debates'.[93] While challenges continue to inhibit gathering such data, oral history can nevertheless provide an opportunity to address this issue. It similarly provides a platform for collecting other absent or muted perspectives – including those conditioned by ethnicity, religion, and sexuality – and the opportunity to integrate them into business history. Janis Thiessen, for example, has interrogated corporate storytelling to argue for a greater focus on the 'historical effects of business on Indigenous peoples and the environment'.[94]

Sharing the Future

As Linda Shopes has noted, the history of oral history tends to be described as a move from understanding interviews as archival documents to understanding them as narrative constructions 'with attendant concerns about memory, subjectivity, and identity that must be interpreted'.[95] This characterisation, she notes, is not misleading but it lacks nuance. Early oral historians certainly engaged with issues concerning memory and subjectivity, while much recent oral history work still largely focuses on adding to and filling out the archive.[96] Nonetheless, identity is becoming a more explicit focus of historians working with oral history. Ronald Kroeze and Jasmijn Vervloet, for example, have recently used interviews to explore intersections between workers' experiences and their company's identity. Stories about company founders were shown to have an influence on the attachment of workers to the company.[97]

Although we have suggested that oral business history evolved separately from mainstream oral history, Shopes' assessment can be applied to it as well – albeit across quite different time frames. The absence of methodological discussions or critiques of interview data until relatively recently does not mean that business historians were oblivious to the nature of their sources. Schooled in social science methodologies, many display a critical awareness of the interview process. And oral history's capacity to fill gaps in the archive and to document specialist knowledge has been and remains a prime motivator for business historians to use it as a tool.[98] But there has also been, belatedly, a more critical engagement with issues of methodology and interpretation – a shift that is part of a discernible sophistication across business history.[99] This book adds to this engagement by offering four case studies of business oral history from Australia. Organised around the themes of disruption and continuity, these demonstrate the versatility and value of oral history for business historians.

The case studies in this book explore the dynamic of creative destruction and the utility of oral history for investigating it. Over the four chapters, we argue that critical engagement with oral history – as a source and a methodological approach – serves to enrich, enhance, and enliven business history as well as its relationship with other historical fields. While our use of Australian case studies reflects our own areas of expertise, our critical engagement with oral history and examination of its possibilities and contribution to business history will nevertheless have universal applications.

Chapter 1 draws on an existing oral history archive that was gathered to produce a corporate history project and made available through a public library. It examines the introduction of supermarkets to Australia, which profoundly disrupted the country's retail landscape during the 1960s. Oral histories with managers, however, show that the development of supermarkets by an established firm could also significantly disrupt its internal dynamics. Drawing on Kanter's conception of shadow organisational power structures, this chapter uses oral histories to examine the ways that power was negotiated within the Coles firm when it pivoted from variety stores to food retailing, starting in the mid-1950s. Interviews also reveal the ways that managers' career ambitions and the demands of the firm clashed with family life. The chapter shows that oral histories offer a unique perspective on organisational culture, managerial power dynamics and work life balance.

Continuity rather than disruption is the central theme of Chapter 2, which examines Australian perceptions of the chocolate manufacturer, Cadbury. Focusing on the relationships between brands and their stakeholders, this chapter considers how different stakeholders viewed the Cadbury brand and its significance over time. Personal, complex, and multifaceted, their responses offer an illuminating insight into the ways that brands are created, articulated, and circulated. In addition to providing access to less tangible aspects of business history, the interviews examined in this chapter also demonstrate that oral history can have practical applications for disciplines beyond history.

Chapter 3 draws on interviews with Australian retail property executives to explore the reasons why shopping centres were able achieve market growth and stability from the 1960s onwards, when retailing itself experienced almost continual disruption. These oral histories show how the industry professionalised as it matured in order to counter negative publicity, improve its profitability, and gain better data to inform development decisions. Listening to these oral histories 'against the grain', however, reveals industry leaders crafting a narrative about the social role of retail property development. In this story, shared across the industry, shopping centres evolved in direct response to the needs of surrounding communities and, in time, became true town centres. Oral history is thus shown to be a multivalanced research methodology, providing nuanced detail about business strategy, while also producing unexpected insights into how narratives are formed and leveraged in business settings.

Chapter 4 explores the disruption caused by the arrival of information technology and digital media within the advertising industry in Australia in the 1990s and 2000s. Interviews with past and current advertising professionals not only offer a first-hand account of the nature of this disruption, but also an opportunity to critically evaluate the narratives contained in other sources – in this case, the trade press. The gradual speed of change outlined by interviewees contrasts with exciting accounts featured in the trade press. Such differences demonstrate the legitimacy of oral history sources and methodologies as well as their capacity to identify, complement, and interrogate other 'conventional' sources.

As these chapters demonstrate, the converging trajectories of business oral history and oral history in recent years offer mutual, beneficial opportunities. For business historians, this intersection provides a means to expand interpretative accounts and to incorporate new methodological approaches. It also reveals the increased possibilities that narrative and memory studies offer, while reiterating the need to consider the collection and analysis of evidence.[100] For oral historians, greater exposure to business historians' oral history accounts offers new perspectives on both methodology and interpretation. The range of sub-disciplines falling under the 'business' umbrella likewise enables business historians to draw on a broad range of methodologies unfamiliar to oral historians. To this end, business history presents a further layer of context to the historical record that has frequently been ignored by mainstream oral historians. As business historians embrace leaders and pioneers on the one hand, and increasingly look beyond and below them on the other, their work reiterates the need for historians to understand both the elite and the marginalised, as well as the interactions between them. Finally, business historians' consideration of the ways that oral history might inform contemporary business practice presents a timely reminder to oral historians and, indeed, all historians that their work performs a key role in connecting the past and the present.

Notes

1 Asher Joel interviewed by Hazel de Berg in the Hazel de Berg collection, 4 June 1973, De B 677, National Library of Australia (NLA).
2 *Ibid.*
3 Adrian Wooldridge, 'Schumpeter: Who's Afraid of Disruption?', *The Economist*, 30 September 2017, https://www.economist.com/business/2017/09/30/whos-afraid-of-disruption.
4 Adrian Wooldridge, *The Great Disruption: How Business is Coping with Turbulent Times* (London: Profile Books, 2015).
5 Richard Gilbert, 'Looking for Mr. Schumpeter: Where Are We in the Competition-Innovation Debate?', *Innovation Policy and the Economy*, 6 (2006): 159.
6 Francisco Louca, 'The Elusive Concept of Innovation for Schumpeter, Marschak and the Early Econometricians', *Research Policy* 43, no. 8 (2014): 1442.
7 Panayotis Michaelides, John Milios, Angelos Vouldis and Spyros Lapatsioras, 'Emil Lederer and Joseph Schumpeter on Economic Growth, Technology and Business Cycles', *Forum for Social Economics* 39, no. 2 (2010): 173.
8 Donald F. Dixon, 'Schumpeter – Fifty Years Later', *Journal of Macromarketing* 20, no. 1 (2000): 84.
9 Joseph Schumpeter, *Capitalism, Socialism and Democracy* (2nd ed.; New York: Harper and Brothers, 1947), 85, quoted in Perry Bliss, 'Schumpeter, the Big Disturbance and Retailing', *Social Forces* 39, no. 1 (1960): 72–76.
10 Joseph Schumpeter, *Capitalism, Socialism and Democracy* (London: Allen & Unwin, 1976), 82–83.
11 Elena Cefis, Franco Malerba, Orietta Marsili and Luigi Orsenigo, 'Time to Exit: "Revolving Door Effect" or "Schumpeterian Gale of Creative Destruction"?', *Journal of Evolutionary Economics* 31, no. 5 (2021): 1469–70.
12 Guido Buenstorf, 'Schumpeterian Incumbents and Industry Evolution', *Journal of Evolutionary Economics* 26, no. 4 (2016): 823–24.
13 Louca, 'The Elusive Concept of Innovation', 1443–44.
14 *Ibid.*
15 *Ibid.*, 1448.
16 Jean-Marie Dru, *Disruption: Overturning Conventions and Shaking Up the Marketplace* (New York: John Wiley & Sons, 1996), back cover.
17 Everett M. Rogers, *Diffusion of Innovations* (New York: Free Press, 2003), 21.

18 D. Hakken, 'Computing and Social Change: New Technology and Workplace Transformation, 1980–1990', *Annual Review of Anthropology* 22, no. 1 (1993): 107.

19 Joseph Schumpeter, *The Theory of Economic Development* (Cambridge, MA: Harvard University Press, 1934), 255, quoted in Dixon, 'Schumpeter – Fifty Years Later', 82–88.

20 David Harvey, *The Enigma of Capital and the Crises of Capitalism* (London: Profile Books, 2010), 46.

21 Barry Bluestone & Bennett Harrison, *The Deindustrialization of America: Plant Closings, Community Abandonment, and the Dismantling of Basic Industry* (New York: Basic Books 1982); Steven C. High, *Industrial Sunset: the Making of North America's Rust Belt, 1969–1984* (Toronto; Buffalo: University of Toronto Press, 2003); Alessandro Portelli, '"This Mill Won't Run No More": Oral History and Deindustrialization', in *New Working-Class Studies*, ed. John Russo and Sherry Lee Linkon (Ithaca, NY: Cornell University Press 2005): 54–62.

22 Michaelides et al., 'Emil Lederer and Joseph Schumpeter', 173.

23 Charles Edquist, ed., *Systems of Innovation: Technologies, Institutions and Organizations* (Pinter, London, 1997); Giovanni Gavetti and Daniel Levinthal, 'Looking Forward and Looking Backward: Cognitive and Experiential Search', *Administrative Science Quarterly* 45, no. 1 (2000): 113–37; Wesley M. Cohen, Akira Goto, Akiya Nagata, Richard R. Nelson and John P. Walsh, 'R&D Spillovers, Patents and the Incentives to Innovate in Japan and the United States', *Research Policy* 31, no. 8 (2002): 1349–67; Franco Malerba, ed. *Sectoral Systems of Innovation* (Cambridge: Cambridge University Press, 2004).

24 Franco Malerba, 'Innovation and the Evolution of Industries', *Journal of Evolutionary Economics* 16, no. 1 (2006): 3–10.

25 *Ibid.*, 7–8.

26 Paul Thompson, *The Voice of the Past* (Oxford: Oxford University Press, 2017), 143.

27 Oral History Society, 'Conference Report – Oral History Society 2013 Conference', cited in Robert Crawford & Matthew Bailey, 'Cousins Once Removed: Revisiting the Relationship between Oral History and Business History', *Enterprise & Society* 20, no. 1 (2019): 5.

28 Robert Perks, 'Corporations are People Too! Business and Corporate Oral History in Britain', *Oral History* 38, no. 1 (Spring, 2010): 36–54.

29 *Ibid.*

30 See Robert Perks, 'The Roots of Oral History: Exploring Contrasting Attitudes to Elite, Corporate, and Business Oral History in Britain and the U.S.', *The Oral History Review* 37, no. 2 (2010): 215–24; Perks, 'Corporations'; Sjoerd Keulen, and Ronald Kroeze, 'Back to Business: A Next Step in the Field of Oral History –The Usefulness of Oral History for Leadership and Organizational Research', *Oral History Review* 39, no. 1 (Winter/Spring 2012): 15–36.

31 Oral History Society, 'Conference Report – Oral History Society 2013 Conference', 5.

32 Donald A. Ritchie, 'Introduction: The Evolution of Oral History', in *The Oxford Handbook of Oral History*, ed. Donald A. Ritchie (New York: Oxford University Press, 2011), 3–22, 3.

33 Cited in Thompson, *The Voice of the Past*, 43–51.
34 Thompson, *The Voice of the Past*, 55–57.
35 Thomson, 'Four Paradigm Transformations', 51; Thompson, *The Voice of the Past*, 48–63.
36 Thomson, 'Four Paradigm Transformations', 51.
37 Thompson, *The Voice of the Past*, 65.
38 John H. Clapham, 'Industrial Organisation in the Woollen and Worsted Industries of Yorkshire', *The Economic Journal* 16, no. 64 (1906): 515–22, 522.
39 Perks, 'Roots', 218–21.
40 Hendry, John. 'The Teashop Computer Manufacturer: J. Lyons, Leo and the Potential and Limits of High-Tech Diversification', *Business History* 29, no. 1 (1987): 73–102; Craig Miner, 'The New Wave, the Old Guard and the Bank Committee: William J. Gred at J. I. Case Company, 1953–1964', *Business History Review*, 61, (Summer 1987): 243–90.
41 Derek Matthews, 'Profit Sharing in the Gas Industry, 1889–1949', *Business History* 30, no. 3 (1988): 306–28, 319–21.
42 Susan Ariel Aaronson, 'Serving America's Business? Graduate business schools and American business, 1945–60', *Business History* 34, no. 1 (1992): 160–80, 170–71.
43 Choi Chi-Cheung, 'Kinship and Business: Paternal and Maternal Kin in Chaozhou Chinese Family Firms', *Business History* 40, no. 1 (1998): 26–49.
44 Patrizia Battilani and Vera Zamagni, 'The Managerial Transformation of Italian Co-operative Enterprises 1946–2010', *Business History* 54, no. 6 (2012): 964–85; Rachel F. Baskerville, 'Professional Closure by Proxy: The Impact of Changing Educational Requirements on Class Mobility for a Cohort of Big 8 Partners', *Accounting History* 11, no. 3 (2006): 290–317, 292.
45 F. K. Boersma, 'Tensions within an Industrial Research Laboratory: the Phillips Laboratory's X-Ray Department between the Wars', *Enterprise & Society* 4, no. 1 (2003): 65–98.
46 Pierre-Antoine Dessaux and Jean-Philippe Mazaud, 'Hybridizing the Emerging European Corporation: Danone, Hachette, and the Divisionalization Process in France during the 1970s', *Enterprise & Society* 7, no. 2 (2006): 227–65.
47 Francesca Carnevali, 'Between Markets and Networks: Regional Banks in Italy', *Business History* 38, no. 3 (1996): 84–100, 95; Ron Berger, David Lamond, Yossi Gavish, and Ram Herstein, 'The Evolution of Management from a Trust to Arm's Length Model in Family Run Businesses: The Case of the Diamond Industry', *Journal of Management History* 22, no. 3 (2016): 341–62.
48 Rachel F. Baskerville, 'Professional Closure by Proxy: The Impact of Changing Educational Requirements on Class Mobility for a Cohort of Big 8 Partners', *Accounting History* 11, no. 3 (2006): 290–317, 292.
49 Frans-Paul van der Putten, 'Corporate Governance and the Eclectic Paradigm: The Investment Motives of Philips in Taiwan in the 1960s', *Enterprise & Society* 5, no. 3 (2004): 490–526, 503; David Stebenne, 'Thomas J. Watson and the Business-Government Relationship, 1933–1956', *Enterprise & Society* 6, no. 1 (2005): 45–75; Helen Shapiro, 'Determinants of

Firm Entry into the Brazilian Automobile Manufacturing Industry, 1956–1968', *Business History Review* 65, no. 4 (1991): 876–947, 892–95; Geoffrey Jones and Andrew Spadafora, 'Creating Ecotourism in Costa Rica, 1970–2000', *Enterprise & Society* 18, no. 1 (2017): 146–83.

50 Mike Parsons and Mary Beth Rose, 'The Neglected Legacy of Lancashire Cotton: Industrial Clusters and the U.K. Outdoor Trade, 1960–1990', *Enterprise & Society* 6, no. 4 (2005): 682–709.

51 Helen Shapiro, 'Determinants of Firm Entry into the Brazilian Automobile Manufacturing Industry, 1956–1968', *Business History Review* 65, no. 4 (1991): 876–947, 885–86.

52 Alan Pilkington, 'Learning from Joint-Venture: The Rover-Honda Relationship', *Business History* 38, no. 1 (1996): 90–114, 108.

53 For recent accounts see Staffan Appelgren, 'History as Business: Changing Dynamics of Retailing in Gothenburg's Second-hand Market', *Business History* 61, no. 1 (2019): 172–86; Ken Sakai, 'Thriving in the Shadow of Giants: The Success of the Japanese Surgical Needle Producer MANI, 1956–2016', *Business History* 61, no. 3 (2019): 429–55; Nicholas Burton, 'The Thatcher Government and (de)Regulation: Modularisation of Individual Personal Pensions', *Journal of Management History* 24, no. 2 (2018): 189–207.

54 Thomson, 'Four Paradigm Transformations', 53.

55 Alistair Thomson, 'Fifty Years On: An International Perspective on Oral History', *The Journal of American History* 85, no. 2 (Sep. 1998): 581–95, 581.

56 Anna Sheftel and Stacey Zembrzycki, 'Who's Afraid of Oral History? Fifty Years of Debates and Anxiety about Ethics', *Oral History Review* 43, no. 2 (2016): 338–66, 340.

57 Sheftel and Zembrzycki, 'Who's Afraid', 341; Thomson, 'Fifty Years On', 581–82.

58 Linda Shopes, '"Insights and Oversights:" Reflections on the Documentary Tradition and the Theoretical Turn in Oral History', *Oral History Review* 41, no. 2 (2014): 257–68, 259.

59 Michelle Emery, Jill Hooks, and Ross Stewart, 'Born at the Wrong Time? An Oral History of Women Professional Accountants in New Zealand', *Accounting History* 7, no. 2 (2002): 7–34; Beverley Lord and Alan Robb, 'Women Students and Staff in Accountancy: The Canterbury Tales', *Accounting History* 15, no. 4 (2010): 529–58; Margaret G. Lightbody, 'Turnover Decisions of Women Accountants: Using Personal Histories to Understand the Relative Influence of Domestic Obligations', *Accounting History* 14, no. 1–2 (2009): 55–78, 59.

60 Emery, Hooks and Stewart, 'Born at the Wrong Time'; Mairi Maclean, Charles Harvey, and Lindsay Stringfellow, 'Narrative, Metaphor and the Subjective Understanding of Historic Identity Transition', *Business History* 59, no. 8 (2017): 1218–41.

61 Robert L. Harrison III, Ann Veeck, and James W. Gentry, 'A Life Course Perspective of Family Meals via the Life Grid Method', *Journal of Historical Research in Marketing* 3, no. 2 (2011): 214–33; Heidi Reed, 'Corporations as Agents of Social Change: A Case Study of Diversity at Cummins Inc.', *Business History* 59, no. 6 (2017): 821–43; Pål Vik, '"The Computer Says No:" The Demise of the Traditional Bank Manager and

the Depersonalisation of British Banking, 1960–2010', *Business History* 59, no. 2 (2017): 231–49.

62 Abe de Jong, David Michael Higgins and Hugo van Driel, 'Towards a New Business History?' *Business History* 57, no. 1 (2017): 5–29; Matthew Bailey 'Snowball sampling in business oral history: accessing and analyzing professional networks in the Australian Property Industry', *Enterprise & Society* 20, no. 1 (2019): 74–88.

63 Thomson, 'Four Paradigm Transformations', 54–55.

64 See Chinmay Tumbe, 'Recent Trends in the Business History of India', *Business History Review* 93, no. 1, 2019): 156; Na Li, 'History, Memory, and Identity: Oral History in China', *The Oral History Review* 47, no. 1 (2020): 37.

65 Lee Parker, 'Historiography for the New Millennium: Adventures in Accounting and Management', *Accounting History* 4, no. 2 (1999): 11–42, 32.

66 Marilyn Collins and Robert Bloom, 'The Role of Oral History in Accounting', *Accounting, Auditing & Accountability Journal* 4, no. 4 (1991): 23–31, 23.

67 *Ibid.*, 30.

68 Theresa Hammond and Prem Sikka, 'Radicalizing Accounting History: The Potential of Oral History', *Accounting, Auditing & Accountability Journal* 9, no. 3 (1996): 79–97, 81.

69 Florian Gebrieter, et al., 'From "Rock Stars" to "Hygiene Factors:" Teachers at Private Accountancy Tuition Providers', *Accounting History* 23, no. 1–2 (2018): 138–50; Lorna Stevenson, David Power, John Ferguson and David Collison, 'The Development of Accounting in UK Universities: An Oral History', *Accounting History* 23, no. 1–2 (2018): 117–37; G. Stevenson Smith, 'Using Oral History Interviews in Accounting Research', *Journal of Accounting and Finance* 19, no. 5 (2019): 151–60.

70 See Keulen and Kroeze, 'Back to Business'; Martyna Śliwa, 'Learning to Listen: An Organizational Researcher's Reflections on "Doing Oral History"', *Management & Organizational History* 8, no. 2 (2013): 185–96.

71 See Robert Crawford and Jackie Dickenson, *Behind Glass Doors: The World of Australian Advertising Agencies*, 1959–1989 (Crawley: UWA Publishing, 2016); Damian Hesse and Katja Lurie, 'The German Advertising Industry – from 1950 to 2018', *Journal of Historical Research in Marketing* 12, no. 1 (2020): 101–125.

72 Robert Crawford, 'Off the Books: Oral History and Transnational Advertising Agencies in Southeast Asia', *Enterprise & Society* 20, no. 1 (2019): 47–59.

73 Andrew Alexander, Dawn Nell, Adrian R. Bailey and Gareth Shaw, 'The Co-creation of a Retail Innovation: Shoppers and the Early Supermarket in Britain', *Enterprise & Society* 10, no. 3 (2009): 529–58, 551–52. See also Adrian R. Bailey, Andrew Alexander and Gareth Shaw, 'Queuing as a Changing Shopper Experience: The Case of Grocery Shopping in Britain, 1945–1975', *Enterprise & Society* 20, no. 3 (2019): 652–83; Robert Crawford and Matthew Bailey, 'Speaking of Research: Oral History and Marketing History', *Journal of Historical Research in Marketing* 10, no. 1 (2018): 107–28.

74 Matthew Bailey, 'Written Testimony, Oral History and Retail Environments: Australian Shopping Centers in the 1960', *Journal of Historical Research in Marketing* 7, no. 3 (2015): 356–72.

75 Andrea Davies and Richard Elliott, 'The Evolution of the Empowered Consumer', *European Journal of Marketing* 40, no. 9/10 (2006): 1106–21, 1107.

76 Terrence H. Witkowski, 'General Book Store in Chicago, 1938–1947: Linking Neighborhood to Nation', *Journal of Historical Research in Marketing* 1, no. 1 (2009): 93–121, 96.

77 Andrea Davies, 'Voices Passed', *Journal of Historical Research in Marketing* 3, no. 4 (2011): 469–85, 480.

78 Ronald K. Mitchell, 'Oral History and Expert Scripts: Demystifying the Entrepreneurial Experience', *Journal of Management History* 2, no. 3 (1996): 50–67.

79 Anna Adorisio Musacchio and Alistair Mutch, 'In Search of Historical Methods', *Management & Organizational History* 8, no. 2, (2013): 105–110, 107.

80 Śliwa, 'Learning to Listen'.

81 Martyna Śliwa and Becky Taylor, '"Everything Comes Down to Money?" Migration and Working Life Trajectories in a (Post-)Socialist Context', *Management & Organizational History* 6, no. 4 (2011): 347–66.

82 Śliwa, 'Learning to Listen', 185, 195.

83 Matthew Hollow and Pål Vik, 'Another Step up the Ladder or Another Foot in the Grave? Re-evaluating the Role of Formal and Informal Training in the Career Development Process within Barclays Bank, 1945–1980', *Management & Organizational History* 11, no. 4 (2016): 345–63; Juha-Antti Lamberg, Sandra Lubinaitė, Jari Ojala and Henrikki Tikkanen, 'The Curse of Agility: The Nokia Corporation and the Loss of Market Dominance in Mobile Phones, 2003–2013', *Business History* 63, no. 4 (2021): 574–605.

84 Christine Wall, 'Something to Show for It: The Place of Mementoes in Women's Oral Histories of Work', *Management & Organizational History* 5, no. 3–4 (2010): 378–94; Andrew Smith and Jason Russell, 'Toward Polyphonic Constitutive Historicism: A New Research Agenda for Management Historians', *Management & Organizational History* 11, no. 2 (2016): 236–51; Mike Zundel, Robin Holt, and Andrew Popp, 'Using History in the Creation of Organizational Identity', *Management & Organizational History* 11, no. 2 (2016): 211–35.

85 Andrew Perchard, Niall G. MacKenzie, Stephanie Decker and Giovanni Favero, 'Clio in the Business School: Historical Approaches in Strategy, International Business and Entrepreneurship', *Business History* 59, no. 6 (2017): 904–27, 915; Mairi Maclean, Charles Harvey and Lindsay Stringfellow, 'Narrative, Metaphor and the Subjective Understanding of Historic Identity Transition', *Business History*, 59, no. 8 (2017): 1218–41.

86 Stephanie Decker, John Hassard and Micheal Rowlinson, 'Rethinking History and Memory in Organization Studies: The Case for Historiographical Reflexivity', *Human Relations*, 74, no. 8 (2020): 1123–55.

87 Vik, 'The Computer'; Andrew Alexander, 'Decision-making Authority in British Supermarket Chains', *Business History* 57, no. 4 (2015): 614–37; Peter Sheldon, Bernard Gan and David Morgan, 'Making Singapore's Tripartism Work (Faster): The Formation of the Singapore National Employers' Federation in 1980', *Business History* 57, no. 3 (2015): 438–60; Maclean, Harvey and Stringfellow, 'Narrative'; Ewean Gibbs,

'The Moral Economy of the Scottish Coalfields: Managing Deindustrialization under Nationalization c.1947–1983', *Enterprise & Society* 19, no. 1 (2018): 124–52.

88 Geoffrey Jones and Rachael Comunale 'Oral History and the Business History of Emerging Markets', *Enterprise & Society* 20, no. 1 (2019): 19–32.

89 Valeria Giacomin, Geoffrey Jones and Erica H. Salvaj, 'Business Investment in Education in Emerging Markets Since the 1960s', *Business History* 63, no. 7 (2021): 1113–43.

90 Ronald Kroeze and Sjoerd Keulen, 'Leading a Multinational is History in Practice: The Use of Invented Traditions and Narratives at AkzoNobel, Shell, Philips and ABN AMRO', *Business History* 55, no. 8 (2013): 1265–87, 1266.

91 John K. Walton, 'New Directions in Business History: Themes, Approaches and Opportunities', *Business History* 52, no. 1 (2010): 1–16, 5–6.

92 Patrick Fridenson, 'Business History and History', in *The Oxford Handbook of Business History*, ed. Geoffrey Jones and Jonathan Zeitlin (Oxford: Oxford University Press, 2007), 9–36, 24.

93 Gabrielle Durepos, Alan McKinlay and Scott Taylor, 'Narrating Histories of Women at Work: Archives, Stories, and the Promise of Feminism', *Business History* 59, no. 8 (2017): 1261–79, 1262.

94 Janis Thiessen, 'The Narrative Turn, Corporate Storytelling, and Oral History: Canada's Petroleum Oral History Project and Truth and Reconciliation Commission Call to Action No. 92', *Enterprise & Society* 20, no. 1 (2019): 70.

95 Linda Shopes, '"Insights and Oversights:" Reflections on the Documentary Tradition and the Theoretical Turn in Oral History', *Oral History Review* 41, no. 2 (2014): 257–68, 259.

96 *Ibid.*, 259–60.

97 Ronald Kroeze and Jasmijn Vervloet, 'A Life at the Company: Oral History and Sense Making', *Enterprise & Society* 20, no. 1 (2019): 33–46.

98 Donald A. Ritchie, 'Introduction: The Evolution of Oral History', in *The Oxford Handbook of Oral History*, ed. Donald A. Ritchie (New York: Oxford University Press, 2011), 3–22, 12.

99 Walter Friedmann and Geoffrey Jones, 'Debating Methodology in Business History', *Business History Review* 91 (Autumn 2017): 443–55.

100 Cheng Gao, Tiona Zuzl, Geoffrey Jones and Tarun Khanna, 'Overcoming Institutional Voids: A Reputation-based View of Long-run Survival', *Strategic Management Journal* 38, no. 1 (2017): 2147–67.

1 Managing Disruption

Business Change, Organisational Politics, and Work Life Balance

In 1956, Thomas North, a young executive from the Australian variety store chain, Coles, was sent by his firm on his first overseas trip. He arrived in the United States with a handful of introductions and a remit to research the latest retail trends for approximately three months. 'Wherever I went I was well received ... [American firms] were prepared to share with you', he later recalled, as he moved across the country,

> perhaps the most significant operational thing [he observed] was these supermarkets. We didn't have them in Australia of course. They impressed me. I couldn't stay out of them, because they were line robbing from the old variety stores ... You could see the old variety stores going backwards while they [the supermarkets] were coming forward. And you talked to people back here and they'd say 'oh they'll never work in Australia, those Supermarkets' ... [But my trip] was the beginning of something that really made me think hard, look down the line into the future ... The first supermarkets we built – they were so wrong. I thought they were magnificent.[1]

Joseph Schumpeter, too, identified the supermarket as a major disruptor. Writing when supermarkets had begun transforming the American landscape, but well before they arrived in Australia, he declared that 'in the case of retail trade the competition that matters arises not from additional shops of the same type, but from the department stores, the chain store, the mail order house and the supermarket'.[2] These retail forms 'mattered' because they transcended familiar forms of competition, creating a 'big disturbance' in the landscape to enforce adaptation by established firms. Supermarkets brought new forms of organisation, new sales-cost relationships, and new methods of selling. The efficiencies of self-service, which included the transfer

DOI: 10.4324/9781003171232-2

of labour from store employees to shoppers, rendered full-service grocery operations uncompetitive on price. And, by applying the same methods to general merchandise, supermarkets also challenged the business models of other retail formats, including variety stores.[3]

While Schumpeter used American retail case studies – observing the role of innovative, emerging firms that rose to rival incumbent operators – the impact of new retail formats spans markets and continents.[4] The department store moved from Europe to America and across the globe. The supermarket arose in America and travelled to Europe, Australia, South America, Asia, and beyond in the decades after the Second World War. Many established firms in these places viewed the United States as a kind of laboratory, a live model market in which innovations were introduced, producing observable disruptions, successes, and failures.[5] Australian firms understood that the supermarket would need to be adapted to local conditions, but both first- and second-mover advantages were on offer to those firms that were prepared to invest in this process. Coles offers a prime example. Although experiments with self-service and primitive supermarkets were underway in Australia, Coles benefited by moving early at a large scale. It also had access to a deep well of information from established American firms that had gone through the learning curve and absorbed the costs of moving first.

The State Library of Victoria, Melbourne, holds a publicly available oral history archive that includes recollections by Coles' managers about their firm's transition into supermarkets. An established archive such as this sets some limits on the historian – there is no opportunity to intervene in the discussion or shape the questions asked – but as Janis Thiessen has argued, it can still contain highly useful data.[6] North's recollection, for example, offers several key insights into the experience of disruption as the supermarket was introduced into Australia. It demonstrates the existential threat faced by variety stores as well as the enthusiasm for change among some managers. It shows the importance of American trends, the congenial relationships between Australian and American firms, and the value attached to American know-how. It also provides an example of the extensive travel undertaken by Coles' managers, which had significant personal and familial implications. Other interviews with Coles' managers unpack these dynamics further. They also demonstrate the challenges and obstacles the firm faced in its turn to food retailing and the deep fissures this caused within Coles, as variety store managers faced declining relevance. The Coles' interviews thus reveal the utility of oral history for providing insights into organisational culture; the messy, complicated process of importing and adapting disruptive innovations to a new market; the political dimensions and power dynamics of organisational relationships; and the challenges of work life balance and how this impacted managers' wives and families. Much of this evidence is unavailable in the written documentary record.

Importing Supermarkets

Grocery chains began forming in Australia in the 1880s and expanded through the first half of the twentieth century. Comprising small, service-oriented stores, they generated some efficiencies of scale, such as buying power, but remained relatively labour-intensive.[7] While self-service had been trialled sporadically in the inter-war years, Australia lacked the necessary packaging, marketing, and logistical infrastructure for it to flourish.[8] Variety stores selling cheap general merchandise were neighbours of these grocery stores in city and suburban high streets across the country. The largest of these, Coles and Woolworths, deployed a 'military' level of organisation to standardise operations, control quality, and to generate efficiencies.[9] Coles started in Victoria in 1914, and Woolworths in New South Wales in 1924. Basing their business models on British and American five and dime stores, their low prices proved popular during the Great Depression. By the early 1950s, both firms had established highly profitable national store networks, and were among the largest retailers in the country. As the decade progressed, however, each became increasingly concerned about the rise of the supermarket in America, and the associate trends observed by Thomas North and other executives.[10]

Supermarkets revolutionised retailing in the United States. They had begun as large self-service food and grocery markets running high-volume, low-price, self-service operations.[11] These stores evolved in conjunction with a range of supporting technologies that included pre-packaged goods, cash registers, shopping trolleys, refrigerators, freezers, new forms of shelving and display, and automobiles.[12] By the fifties, supermarkets were highly rationalised retail forms, with the largest chains employing professional managers who applied systems to all aspects of operations.[13] Before the Second World War, senior directors in Coles had believed that 'no one's ever going to make money out of groceries'.[14] Opinions shifted after the war as Australian firms observed international developments with a mixture of excitement and alarm.

Roy Dallimore, Chief Accountant and Finance Director for Coles in the 1960s and 1970s, recalled that after Managing Director, Edgar Coles, visited America in the mid-1950s, he returned and gave a presentation at the firm's head office entitled 'Tomorrow's Newspaper' in which he argued that 'we had to get into food'.[15] Edgar's son, Robert Coles, remembered that his father returned convinced that 'the writing was on the wall for variety stores'.[16] 'Almost within twenty four hours', Edgar dispatched his trusted lieutenant, Lance Robinson to America. 'It was as urgent as that... because he could see [Coles] were getting left behind in the race' to develop food retailing.[17] The turn to food was, in part, because the firm had already saturated Australia with variety stores, whereas 'there was an unlimited future with supermarkets'.[18] Moreover, as Thomas North had observed, supermarkets also sold much of the general merchandise stocked by variety stores, but did so more efficiently with cheaper prices. Coles chose to cannibalise its own sales rather than lose market share to a rival firm.

Some managers felt very confident about the future of supermarkets:

> You felt all along that if you had been to America that it was something that was going to take place. We seemed to follow the American pattern... there was no reason why it [the supermarket] shouldn't be good in Australia. People are just people.[19]

Others were less sure: 'have no doubt there were certain executives who felt [supermarkets] may not work'.[20] F. L. Thompson, who owned one of the country's largest grocery chains, also believed that supermarkets would 'never succeed in Australia'.[21] Coles acquired his firm, kept its supply chains, garnered expertise from its managers, and used its retail footprint to expand interstate before closing down most of its small stores that the new supermarkets rendered obsolete. The Thompson takeover was representative of the approach adopted by both Coles and their chief rival Woolworths. With little experience selling food, Coles' senior management looked to acquire expertise by taking over established grocery chains.[22] Some of these had begun to implement self-service, but few had developed anything approaching the modern supermarket. The takeovers took Coles ahead 'in leaps and bounds ... and stimulated development no end'.[23]

Internal Organisational Disruption

The acquisition of rival firms brought a clash of cultures. One manager recalls that:

> The company had decided to buy [the grocery chain] Dickens and it wasn't a popular thing from the guys, like me, who were out in

the stores because Dickens were a bit of a pain in the neck to us [because you get] a bit cranky with the guy down the street, whoever he might be, that's underselling you.[24]

The Dickens employees, for their part, 'didn't like [being acquired] one little bit' either.[25] Nor did office staff in other chains that Coles took over.[26] So while Coles retained many store staff in acquired firms, office staff and managers often found the change too confronting and left. Those whose skills were valued had to be convinced to stay. Lance Robinson recalls telling two managers who were planning on leaving:

> You're very foolish gentlemen ... you'll find we're a very good company to work for ... you'll have a hell of a time for the first twelve months but don't let that worry you ... you've got knowledge. We want that knowledge. And we'll upset you because we want you to do it our way ... We only have one way and that's our way ... we don't debate ... but I believe we will be wise enough to use your skills.[27]

Robinson aimed to compel retention but instead articulated the reasons why the managers decided to leave: Coles' way of doing business, their organisational approach, and working culture were immediately exerted on acquired firms. Murray Fraser, who was appointed the Secretary of the S. E. Dickens chain shortly after Coles acquired it, and before it was rebadged under the Coles' banner, recalls that:

> the fellow I replaced [in Dickens]... had an office with opaque glass in it and he got in there and he lit a cigarette and it just hung on his lip until it burnt out and then he lit another one and he opened all the mail himself. Every bit of mail would be piled high. And the first thing I did was to get rid of the opaque glass and let people see what was going on in the office and let someone else open the mail.[28]

Jim Thomas, a Coles' accountant, claims that he 'would spend days arguing with their accounting people [in the Queensland Penney's chain] that there was a need for this system and these were the reasons why I believed our way of doing it was better'.[29] Many of the arguments were about 'trivial' processes such as how postage stamps were purchased and used, but could occupy significant time as Coles' managers 'fought every inch of the way' to introduce new processes.[30]

Coles' Organisational Shadow Structure

In Kanter's sociological study of a large American multi-national, she noted that employees and managers were keenly aware of organisational politics. It formed a frequent topic of conversation, was understood to shape careers, inform strategy, and affect productivity. 'Somewhere behind the formal organization chart', she wrote, 'was another, shadow structure in which dramas of power were played out'.[31] The shadow structure does not come attached to the organisational structure in documentary archives. Traces of it may emerge, however, in oral histories. Bevan Bradbury told his interviewer that

> anyone who looks at the history of a company and doesn't examine internal politics is only kidding themselves because the internal politics is the dominant influence, and it reaches a stage where [it becomes] ... a nightmare. I was fighting two battles. Two full blooded battles at one time.

The first was to get Coles' supermarkets running efficiently and profitably. The second was dealing with the internal opposition to this endeavour, grappling with

> all the baying and yapping that was going on ... you know 'disaster, disaster' ... It was like saying to a general ... 'you planned this battle and now you've got some casualties in the first few minutes so it's a disaster, disaster.' Of course, you've got casualties. It's what bloody casualties are for ... In this case gross profit was the casualty.[32]

Supermarkets proved to be a defining and highly successful strategic turn for Coles, as well as its rival Woolworths. But they were not welcomed by many within the organisation because of the internal disruption they sparked and the power shifts they instigated.[33] Oral histories in which participants articulate their understanding of this disruption thus add fine-grained detail and internal organisational context to Schumpeter's broader concept of disruptive innovation. When Coles' executives decided to import the supermarket model, their firm became an active participant in the 'gale of innovation' sweeping through post-war Australian retailing. The force of this gale can be measured using retail sales data, the decline of independent grocery stores, increasing grocery sales per head of population, and the growing floor space devoted to food retailing.[34] Its influence on the fortunes of Coles itself can be similarly quantified by charting sales growth, customer numbers, and market share. Its impact on the firm's political shadow structure, however, while strongly felt throughout the organisation, remains elusive without qualitative data such as oral history.

Bradbury's claims about the battles he fought to establish the supermarket selling methods can be seen, on the one hand, as an effort to sustain his own legend about the man responsible for the success of Coles' supermarket project. As Clarke et al. argue, managers and employees constantly seek to author their own narratives, to make sense of their work and inscribe it with meaning.[35] Even with oral histories, we cannot know all the nuances of the organisational politics within Coles, nor should we accept Bradbury's testimony uncritically. But his interview, in conjunction with the reflections of other managers, offers us a glimpse of Coles' shadow structure and a sense of the power contest that accompanied supermarket development. A new organisational hierarchy destabilised Coles' shadow structure because resources were allocated to promote the growth of the grocery operation and produce an internal competitor to variety stores. Variety store managers, like their stores, experienced declining relevance. Some saw the opportunities in food and embraced the new path. Others offered covert or overt resistance.

The early organisational reticence towards selling groceries was evident in the approach taken after Coles took over the Queensland Penney's chain in 1956. The Penney's stores operated as hybrid variety grocery shops. Coles executives charged with managing the Penney's stores actually removed most of their food offer and pushed what was left to the back of the stores because the 'margins on food were so low'.[36] This upset managers of the original firm who believed that it was a significant mistake.[37] One executive involved in the process described the resulting shop as 'a very labour intensive supermarket' that used a small food offer to 'sell the high markup [variety] merchandise' that occupied much of the store.[38] In many of the stores 'where we threw food out, we went back years later and it cost us an enormous amount of money to put in [food-oriented] supermarkets'.[39]

The strategy with Penney's can be seen as the cost of developing new capabilities, but there was also politically motivated internal opposition that created obstacles to supermarket development. Many managers who had built careers working their way up the variety store hierarchy, and who defined themselves through their capabilities in the field, felt deep animosity towards the new food operation. Brian Quinn who worked on both sides of the firm through his career ascension to Managing Director and Chairman of the company suggested that for these variety store managers: 'their kingdom, as it were ... they could see it crumbling and breaking up'.[40] Because the supermarkets were 'line-robbing' from the variety stores, the relationship between the divisions became 'very political'.[41] Some variety supervisors when instructed to go into supermarkets and train staff in general merchandise marketing 'wouldn't go near the [supermarkets]'.[42] When variety managers were forced to send their people in, 'they wouldn't supply anybody but the worst. They wouldn't supply the best because it was them and us'.[43] The early supermarkets were 'filled with blokes who weren't good enough to run a little variety store'.[44] Variety executives also objected to supplying goods to their new internal competitor. One executive recalls variety store buyer and Associate Director, George McGowen, arguing that 'any silly bugger can sell groceries but they're not bright enough to buy and sell variety. Why should we give them all our [general merchandise] stuff and let them mishandle it, cut the price and eat away our margins'.[45] 'George was violently opposed to [the supermarkets] and so was practically everybody in Coles'.[46] Even in the late 1960s, an 'us and them' situation continued, with management still trying to make the variety division realise that food was 'a part of the empire rather than just a poor relation'.[47]

Variety store managers who embraced the turn to food, however, found it 'exciting [and] demanding. Every day it was different and of course you're selling fresh produce and meat, delicatessen merchandise and, of course, groceries'.[48] And despite the challenges they faced learning the new art of grocery merchandising, the lack of operational knowledge within Coles opened opportunities for rapid career ascension. Bevan Bradbury was a case in point. When he was sent to Maitland in regional New South Wales to open a supermarket, one of his first challenges was to deal with massive flooding in the area. He made his reputation by finding a boat and personally ferrying goods out of the flooded supermarket to salvage stock. Managers from the time also recall him getting into the 'hack work' of packing shelves when underperforming early supermarkets were pruned of staff.[49] These examples demonstrate the reputational power of narrative within firms. Bradbury's legend travelled through informal and formal networks inside Coles, marking him for promotion. Again, this was a process observed by Kanter – employees in her study were keenly aware of who was identified for career advancement. It was a topic of conversation and part of the collective knowledge of the firm. People on 'fast tracks' had a profile within the company even before they held senior positions.[50] The story about Bradbury salvaging goods from his flooded store was retold

within the firm, attaching to his person several highly prized characteristics: determination, inventiveness, company loyalty, and an ability to
overcome challenges. With the early supermarket operation in disarray,
these traits marked him as an ideal candidate to right the ship.

Applying Systems: 'Nobody Knows Quite What is Best to Do'[51]

The opposition Bradbury and other proponents of supermarkets faced
was clearly informed by issues of identity and disruptions to organisational power. But many variety managers also simply did not understand the underlying principles of the low-margin, high-turnover
supermarket model. This sacrificed the markup on individual goods
to potentially produce high net profits – if efficient systems could
be applied at scale. Although Bradbury had been trained in variety
stores, he understood and embraced this logic, which was the basis
of the mass-market, self-service model. Looking back after serving
as the Managing Director of Coles in the 1980s, he argued that the
early supermarket group ran 'like a two-bob watch' because it was
'surrounded by variety [store] thinking'.[52] Early on, he said,

> all the managers that came into the [food] operation were general
> merchandise or variety store managers and they just didn't under-
> stand food ... [they] tried variety concepts and it just didn't work ...
> The overheads were such that we were just totally uncompetitive.[53]

The scale and high stock turnover inherent in supermarket operations
meant that many established variety store processes needed to be
adapted or abandoned. David Guild, who spent most of his career at
senior levels in the variety division, recalls that in variety stores:

> Everything that came in had to be recorded in the storeman's
> book ... You imagine it with food when you get twenty tonnes of
> groceries ... The man would spend all of his day writing... it's such
> a volume business.[54]

Jim McKenzie, former Controller of Methods and Systems, notes
that after the storeman recorded incoming goods, 'the office girl
wrote everything in detail in the invoice book and ... from that she
kept shrinkage sheets and markdown sheets and markup sheets'.[55]
McKenzie's recollections reveal an unquestioned gendered division of
labour at the time as well as the costs of replicating Coles' manual

stock-taking systems in volume-oriented food stores. McKenzie noted that you 'couldn't afford the control' or rigour of the old variety store processes. In variety stores, 'every counter had to provide so many pounds, shillings and pence in sales for a week – you couldn't apply that to a [supermarket] gondola'.[56]

Coles' variety store systems were highly regimented. Managers 'knew exactly what to do in every situation'. Unable to apply these to the new world of food, many were left to learn by trial and error: 'suddenly you're thrown into this ... [and] a lot of it you had to find your own way, make your own rules ... It was a difficult transition'.[57] When managers moved interstate, they could find themselves dealing with new systems and processes inherited from grocery chains acquired there.[58] Without standardised systems, there was wide variation between stores producing inefficiencies and stress. With staff, buyers, and managers all finding their own way, 'it was a case, almost, of the blind leading the blind'.[59]

With the food operation struggling, Bradbury was dispatched to America, where 'he spent three or four months ... getting experience ... mostly with Krogers'[60] in 'a hands-on situation [learning] how to run these things'.[61] The Kroger Grocery & Baking Company was founded in the 1880s, grew to one of America's largest grocery chains by the 1930s, and moved into supermarkets in the 1950s.[62] Like other supermarket operators in the United States, it exerted heavy price competition on variety stores. Upon his return, Bradbury recalled, Edgar Coles 'kept the variety people at bay'. He argues that

> those people would have ruined the company, ruined the food operation had they been allowed to do so ... People like me ... were struggling like hell to try and introduce supermarkets into Coles using supermarket and food ways, which are very lean, hungry, close to the bone, low gross profit, high turnover ... which is the very antithesis of the variety store at the time.

He claimed that had Edgar Coles not separated the two arms of the company, 'we would never have got the Supermarket Division off the ground because it would have been overburdened and weighed down with costly expenses'.[63] Robert Coles declared that the new division was a way of 'sort of putting up a sign saying this was "Supermarket! Variety keep out"'.[64]

Over time, systems were developed.[65] These drew on knowledge acquired from America, the food expertise of those managers who had worked in grocery chains acquired by Coles and who chose to stay, and trial and error experiments in store. Jim McKenzie, who was charged with developing these systems, claimed that 'we were changing every single thing to make it more efficient'.[66] 'Thousands of memos' were summarised, and organised into a routine handbook, sections of which remained in use for decades.[67] Archival records provide evidence of the end results of this process, but there is little documentation of the frustrations, errors, wrong turns, and labour invested in developing the early supermarket systems. Oral histories again fill these gaps. They reveal, for example, problems that have been reported in other markets during the nascent phase of supermarket development.[68] These included immature supporting technologies as well as car parking shortages. Robert Coles noted that the entire supermarket system 'all depended on packaging. You see the American packaging systems were so far advanced... whereas packaging systems in Australia hadn't got that far along the track'.[69] The provision of car parking became a key challenge for all shops by the late 1950s and the subject of lobbying efforts by the larger retailers.[70] Coles, even as it was building car parking into its new developments, also dispatched representatives to local councils and retail bodies. They lectured these groups on the 'virtues of developing off-street parking in their shopping areas... the message was: "get your off-street parking or this shopping centre will not survive"'.[71]

The move to perishable items was another of the big challenges mentioned by several executives.[72] As one noted, 'stock-taking for food and perishables is a totally different exercise'.[73] One of the reasons Coles acquired grocery chains was to gain buying power and food retailing knowledge. Executives from firms like Penny's and S. E. Dickens helped supply the latter, but many gaps remained. Managers who were moved from variety to food faced a steep learning curve:

> I, you know, went through some fairly embarrassing times trying to work out the difference between ham and shoulder. I didn't really know where the various different cuts of meat came from. I had to go out to the abattoirs and talk to them out there... Really you learn the hard way... I guess that I had sufficient common sense and a bit of luck, I guess, to survive the first couple of years while you picked it up.[74]
> We didn't know too much about meat. You're into hens and specialists to a large degree there and gross profits in those departments could fluctuate quite wildly.[75]

Most suppliers had more experience and deeper professional networks than the executives charged with engaging them. Variety store manager,

Graeme Seabrook, was sent to Queensland in the early 1960s to become the food buyer for Queensland supermarkets and found an informal supplier's group that exerted price standardisation on retail stores.

> Before the Trade Practices Act came in, all the small goods suppliers had got together and agreed on prices and all the various retailers were charged a fixed price ... It was quite a skill to try and get in and break up the cartel ... The way that we did that was ... say there were four major suppliers. They each expected to get a quarter of the business, so we pushed one guy to the side and didn't give him any and transferred a lot of the business to another guy and they started looking at each other. And this guy is saying, 'Well how come I've lost the business and he's picked it up if his price is the same.' So this [other] guy couldn't believe his luck because he wasn't giving us anything initially and the guy who'd lost the business would come in and say, 'Well, I can see that I'm missing out here.' And he would give us a rebate, which we would then accept and then one of the other guys would lose the business, and slowly but surely the price cartel broke down and then it would go into a price war from there.[76]

American know-how again proved valuable. Jim McKenzie, who ran Coles' systems, visited America and 'was taken out in Chicago to the A & P Food Company'. He said, 'I learnt an awful lot in that store ... They were the biggest retailer in the U.S.A., [with] fantastically good [manual] systems ... [which] when we got into grocery, I was able to use'.[77] Using the A&P system allowed Coles to turn around a stock order in 48 hours, compared to the ten days it took Woolworths, which used a primitive punch card system. McKenzie also claimed to have improved on the American accounting systems. 'We could do ... the whole company result in three weeks, and the Yanks used to come out and it took them three months, and they said, Look we've got $10,000,000 worth of computers and we can't do this'.[78] The claim of improving on American know-how was not uncommon in Australian retailing. Early shopping centres were also sometimes described as an upgrade on the American model from which they were derived. This was a way of coding adaptations to retail forms that were shaped by local conditions.

The Family Life of Managers

Andrews et al. argue that oral histories 'provide insights into the negotiation of everyday social life'.[79] The evidence discussed above regarding the internal political dynamics of the firm is one example of this. But interviews with Coles' executives also at times branched out into discussions about family life, revealing some of the personal implications of the supermarket disruption for those tasked with managing its course in Australia. What becomes clear is that the structural changes supermarkets necessitated within the firm had significant implications for the private lives of its managers. The development of national supermarket chains; the need for state-based organisation; layers of supervision; research departments; systems innovation; property development divisions; marketing teams; and new finance and accounting capabilities advanced the spread of the managerial revolution in post-war Australia. A wide literature in the United States at the time explored this new career path, the 'new middle class [it] created', the men it produced and even their family lives.[80]

Managers, according to Goffee and Scase, worked 'within hierarchies where pay, promotion, and security – and associated enhancements in status and responsibility – were major incentives'.[81] Other researchers suggested that these managers internalised the work ethic required to prosecute their firm's goals to the point that it became their central life interest.[82] The middle-class career, Ely Chinoy declared, offered the manager 'a career pattern which channels his aspirations and sustains his hope'.[83] Several Coles' managers expressed views that appear to reflect this dynamic. Thomas North started his career working in Coles' stores at the end of the Second World War and rose through the ranks to become the Managing Director and Chairman of the company in the late 1970s and early 1980s. Extolling the virtues of his firm, he later declared that: 'I always believed that if you gave the company everything ... they would look after you'.[84] Many others described Coles as their 'family'.[85] 'I put my life into it', said one, 'but you had the security – they'd look after you... [and] then it was [down to] how hard you worked'.[86]

At a basic level, the growth of supermarkets opened opportunities for more men to pursue corporate careers within Coles and other retail firms. It also necessitated a deep investment of labour time and geographic mobility among its managerial ranks. When Coles needed managers to relocate, they 'were just told' where and when to move. Such demands had been imposed on variety store managers, but the scale of supermarket development generated even greater demand for geographic mobility, which came to form the spine of career paths: at each new location, responsibility was extended, experience expanded, commitment and competence tested. Such travel was common, not only for senior executives, but for store managers, too, who were 'shifted all around Australia'. These relocations were imposed from above but by linking them to career progression, Coles incentivised managers to make personal sacrifices and invest heavily in the firm. Kanter has termed this process 'the seductiveness of opportunity' – a self-reinforcing progression in which career advancement breeds ambition and a desire for further advancement.[87] The experiences of Coles' managers then, while unusual in terms of the amount of travel required, position them within a post-war managerial class in Australia that was enculturated to accept personal costs as a trade for career advancement.[88]

'As "organizational men" [Coles] managers were expected to adhere to work values that gave priority to corporate demands over other interests – including those of their immediate families'.[89] Wilf Coles began his 50-year career with Coles as a store salesman and ended it as a Company Director. In one particularly torrid stretch during the 1950s, he moved in short succession from Melbourne, Victoria, to the humid river town of Maryborough on Queensland's Fraser Coast, to the dry steppe climate of Mildura in regional Victoria, to the densely populated beach suburbs of eastern Sydney, to Launceston, 900 miles south in Tasmania, and then to Perth, in Western Australia. His wife and children moved with him agreeably, until the latter grew older and became resistant to breaking teenage friendships. The family remained in Perth for seven years, although Wilf Coles was still constantly travelling within the state in his new role of store supervisor. Despite his frequent absences, he and his family connected to local networks and created deep friendship groups, particularly through a strong interest in sailing which they developed while living in Perth. 'The only time I've ever seen my kids cry', Coles recalled, 'was when they had to shift from Perth'.[90] Another executive who advanced consistently claimed to have made 13 moves in 11 years, but contextualised the challenges of this within his personal experience: 'We had to take it. You see, I got married [when I was unemployed and] out of work. I was lucky to get into Coles, very lucky. And thank God I did. And I never looked back'.[91]

As these examples demonstrate, a managerial career was heavily dependent on domestic support, particularly as the corporate man was required to be more mobile and work longer hours than managers of previous generations.[92] This was impossible without the unpaid labour of the executive wife, and so she became an object of interest for both corporations and researchers. In the United States, the latter identified duties and responsibilities such as keeping the home running smoothly, taking care of children, entertaining, and allocating time for one's husband. The executive's wife was also required to be 'adaptable in meeting new people and constantly changing situations', not least because her husband's career progression could well require her to relocate to other cities.[93] One English study in the mid-sixties even found managers who vetted potential marriage partners based on their preparedness to relocate to support their career. Failure to comply was 'a black mark' because it set a limit on the male manager realising 'his full potential'.[94]

Coles' managers did not articulate this compact so starkly in their oral history interviews, but did express an awareness of the familial disruption resulting from careers committed to the firm. And they all understood that relocation was a requirement for career advancement. Coles' managers who would not or could not relocate suffered the consequences. One who refused to leave Victoria for family reasons was told by senior management that his 'inability to move virtually curtail[ed] his career'.[95] One executive completed an agreed three-year stint in Sydney and asked to be returned to Melbourne on compassionate grounds. Despite being recognised for his good work, he was placed in an undesirable role in the records department as 'penance ... because in those days it wasn't the done thing to ask to go back'[96] – especially if the head office wanted a manager to continue in a role that served the company's interests.

Writing in the 1970s, Kanter warned against corporate-wife-as-victim analyses that failed to appreciate the agency of women in supporting roles, but noted that 'no one disagreed that marriage to successful men was constraining, shaped role demands for wives, and often put the family last in the men's priorities'.[97] She described manager's wives having the 'boundaries of their own life choices set by the company'.[98] The wife of one Coles' executive interjected during his interview, which was recorded at their home: 'I was a bit of a rebel to the cause', she said.

> Because when we were moved from Brisbane to Adelaide, my children were in a pretty vital stage of their schooling ... towards the end of the year. And I just said I wasn't moving until they had finished ... Well of course that caused a bit of an uproar, because they weren't used to wives saying they weren't going... they just didn't believe that the family were important... I had a very old Queensland friend... who used to say "I've never heard a Coles wife who doesn't complain." They were in the main fairly unhappy. Because [Coles]... would move men with no thought [about the effect] that would have on their children.[99]

When a Coles' manager was moved interstate, some wives gave up careers to move the family with them.[100] 'Leaving Sydney and going to South Australia was rather traumatic for the family', noted one manager. 'It was like going to the other side of the world... It was tough on [my wife] because she was home all day. We had two young children at the time'. Their extended family and support structures remained far behind in Sydney.[101]

In some cases, family social life also revolved around Coles. In his interview, Harry Boyce declared that the 'social life was magnificent. We just lived and talked and loved Coles ... Always Coles. We didn't know anyone outside'. Boyce remembered

> there were six fellows in Coles and their wives would come to our place on a Saturday night and we'd have a few beers and play roulette and then we'd go the following week to another one's home. And those friends were all Coles men. And the wives were left sitting over there, and the men were talking Coles, Coles and Coles. And that's 24 hours a day. And that was every day and every weekend. So, it was a wonderful atmosphere.[102]

There is no record of Mrs Boyce's experience of this environment, but the firm was clearly the centre of gravity.

*** *** ***

Supermarkets, as a technology and system for selling food and general merchandise, represented a gale of disruption in Australia from the mid-1950s onwards. Coles internalised and harnessed the innovation, contributing to a wave of retail modernisation that transformed the country's retail landscape during the post-war boom. In doing so, it rendered obsolete its own chain of variety stores that had been its core business since inception in 1914. Oral histories provide a unique opportunity to observe the internal dynamics of the firm during this sharp and radical transition. They reveal the perspectives of those observing and participating in decisions that re-made the company, providing evidence of failed attempts to adapt and the processes by which these were overcome. They offer a glimpse of the political shadow structure that lay behind the official organisational hierarchy and the ways that this was disrupted by the upheaval required to develop supermarkets. Recognising these power dynamics, as Coles' managers noted, is absolutely critical to understanding the development of the firm as it grappled with the challenges of introducing an entirely new type of retailing on a mass-market scale over a short time frame. The pressures and costs borne by male managers who participated in this process flowed on to their families and personal relationships. By recording the human dimensions of innovative disruption and the introduction of 'the competition that matters', oral histories provide nuance and complexity to these developments and offer business history new and exciting areas of enquiry.

Notes

1 Thomas North, interview by Stella Barber, 13 January 1986, Box 4764, Coles Myer Archive, State Library of Victoria (hereafter CMA, SLV).
2 Joseph Schumpeter, *Capitalism, Socialism and Democracy* (New York: Harper & Row, 1950), 85.
3 Perry Bliss, 'Schumpeter, The "Big" Disturbance and Retailing', *Social Forces* 39, no. 1 (1960): 72.
4 Victoria de Grazia, *Irresistible Empire: America's Advance Through 20th-century Europe* (Cambridge, MA: Belknap Press, 2005); Andrew Alexander, Simon Phillips and Gareth Shaw, 'Retail Innovation and Shopping Practices: Consumers' Reactions to Self-Service Retailing', *Environment and Planning A* 40, no. 9 (2008): 2204–221.
5 Matthew Bailey, *Managing the Marketplace: Reinventing Shopping Centres in Post-War Australia* (Routledge: London, 2020), 22–40; Lydia Langer, 'How West German Retailers Learned to Sell to a Mass Consumer Society', in *Transformations of Retailing in Europe after 1945*, ed. Lydia Langer, Ralph Jessen, and Gareth Shaw (Farnham; Burlington, VT: Ashgate, 2012), 71–85, 77–78.
6 Janis Thiessen, 'The Narrative Turn, Corporate Storytelling, and Oral History: Canada's Petroleum Oral History Project and Truth and Reconciliation Commission Call to Action No. 92', *Enterprise & Society* 20, no. 1 (2019): 60–73.
7 Kim Humphery, *Shelf Life: Supermarkets and the Changing Cultures of Consumption* (Cambridge, Melbourne: Cambridge University Press, 1998), 52; No author, 'Cato, Frederick John', *Australian Dictionary of Biography* (Canberra: National Centre of Biography, Australian National University), https://adb.anu.edu.au/biography/cato-frederick-john-5533/text9425; Beverley Kingston, *Basket, Bag and Trolley: A History of Shopping in Australia* (Melbourne: Oxford University Press, 1994).
8 John S. Ewing, 'Marketing in Australia', *Journal of Marketing* 26, no. 2 (1962): 56; Kingston, *Basket, Bag and Trolley*, 86; De Grazia, *Irresistible Empire*, 385.
9 Michael Kelly, interview with Jenny Hudson, 27 September 1996, transcript, 3, State Library of NSW (SLNSW), MLOH 451, nos. 58, 59 & 60.
10 David T. Merrett, 'The Making of Australia's Supermarket Duopoly, 1958–2000', *Australian Economic History Review* 60, no. 30 (2020): 306–307.
11 Chester H. Liebs, *Main Street to Miracle Mile: American Roadside Architecture*, 2nd ed. (Baltimore: Johns Hopkins University Press, 1995),

123–27; David Appel, 'The Supermarket: Early Development of an Institutional Innovation', *Journal of Retailing* 48, no. 1 (1972): 43.

12 Walter Y. Oi, 'The Supermarket: An Institutional Innovation', *The Australian Economic Review* 37, no. 3 (2004): 338.

13 Patrick Hyder Patterson, 'The Supermarket as a Global Historical Development', in *The Routledge Companion to the History of Retailing*, ed. Jon Stobart and Vicki Howard (Abingdon; New York: Routledge, 2019), 156–58; Andrew Alexander, Dawn Nell, Adrian R. Bailey, and Gareth Shaw, 'The Co-Creation of a Retail Innovation: Shoppers and the Early Supermarket in Britain', *Enterprise & Society* 10, no. 3 (2009): 529–58; De Grazia, *Irresistible Empire*, 377–85; Andrew Alexander and Simon Phillips, 'Retail Innovation and Shopping Practices: Consumers' Reactions to Self-Service Retailing', *Environment and Planning A* 40, no. 9 (2008): 2209; Frank Trentmann, *Empire of Things: How We Became a World of Consumers, from the Fifteenth Century to the Twenty-First* (New York: HarperCollins, 2017), 348.

14 Tom Morgans, interview by Stella Barber, 5 March 1987, Box 4768, CMA, SLV.

15 Roy Dallimore, interview by Stella Barber, 14 March 1986, Box 4764, CMA, SLV. See also, Stella M. Barber, 'Coles, Sir Edgar Barton (1899–1981)', *Australian Dictionary of Biography* (Canberra: National Centre of Biography, Australian National University), https://adb.anu.edu.au/biography/coles-sir-edgar-barton-18063/text22157

16 Robert Coles, interview by Stella Barber, 6 May 1986, Box 4765, CMA, SLV.

17 David Guild, interview by Stella Barber, 3 October 1986, Box 4765, CMA, SLV.

18 R. Coles, interview.

19 Wilfred Coles, interview by Stella Barber, 21 February 1986, Box 4764, CMA, SLV.

20 Thomas North, interview by Stella Barber, 3 October 1985, Box 4763, CMA, SLV.

21 Thomas North, interview by Stella Barber, 11 October 1985, Box 4763, CMA, SLV.

22 Merrett, 'The Making of Australia's Supermarket Duopoly', 307–308.

23 Thomas North, interview by Stella Barber, 12 December 1985, Box 4764, CMA, SLV.

24 Geoff Coulson, interview by Emma Harrold, 5 March 1996, Box 4750, CMA, SLV.

25 Murray Fraser, interview by Stella Barber, 26 May 1994, Box 4749, CMA, SLV.

26 Raymond Schlecht, interview by Stella Barber, 28 June 1986, Box 4765, CMA, SLV; Neil Thornton, interview by Emma Harold, 22 January 1996, Box 4750, CMA, SLV.

27 Lance Robinson, interview by Stella Barber, 21 November 1985, Box 4763, CMA, SLV.

28 Fraser, interview, 26 May 1994.

29 Jim Thomas, interview by Stella Barber, 9 December 1987, Box 4766, CMA, SLV.

30 *Ibid.*

31 Rosabeth Moss Kanter, *Men and Women of the Corporation* (New York: Basic Books, 1977), 164–65.
32 Bevan Bradbury, interview by Stella Barber, 6 April 1988, Box 4768, CMA, SLV.
33 Merrett, 'The Making of Australia's Supermarket Duopoly', 310.
34 *Ibid.*; Matthew Bailey, 'Retail Suburbanization, Modernization, and Growth in Sydney During Australia's Postwar Boom', *Journal of Urban History* (2021: E-pub ahead of print); Matthew Bailey, 'Absorptive Capacity, International Business Knowledge Transfer, and Local Adaptation: Establishing Discount Department Stores in Australia', *Australian Economic History Review* 57, no. 2 (2017): 194–216.
35 Caroline A. Clarke, Andrew D. Brown and Veronica Hope Hailey, 'Working Identities? Antagonistic Discursive Resources and Managerial Identity', *Human Relations* 62, no. 3 (2009): 323–52.
36 Jim McKenzie, interview by Stella Barber, 7 April 1988, Box 4768, CMA, SLV.
37 Raymond Schlecht, interview by Stella Barber, 28 June 1986, Box 4765, CMA, SLV.
38 David Guild, interview by Stella Barber, 3 October 1986, Box 4765, CMA, SLV.
39 *Ibid.*
40 Brian Quinn, interview by Stella Barber, 23 December 1987, Box 4765, CMA, SLV.
41 Graeme Seabrook, interview by Stella Barber, 24 March 1988, Box 4768, CMA, SLV.
42 Guild, interview.
43 McKenzie, interview, 7 April 1988.
44 Jim McKenzie, interview by Stella Barber, 14 April 1988, Box 4767, CMA, SLV.
45 *Ibid.*
46 *Ibid.*
47 Graeme Seabrook, interview by Stella Barber, 3 May 1988, Box 4769, CMA, SLV.
48 Russell Stucki, interview by Stella Barber, 7 April 1988, Box 4768, CMA, SLV. See also, Guild, interview; Seabrook, interview.
49 Jim Thomas, interview by Stella Barber, 16 December 1987, Box 4766, CMA, SLV.
50 Kanter, *Men and Women of the Corporation*, 133–36.
51 Lance Robinson, interview by Stella Barber, 22 November 1985, Box 4763, CMA, SLV.
52 Bevan Bradbury, interview by Stella Barber, 6 April 1988, Box 4768, CMA, SLV.
53 Guild, interview.
54 *Ibid.*
55 McKenzie, interview, 14 April 1988.
56 Guild, interview.
57 Stucki, interview.
58 *Ibid.*
59 *Ibid.*
60 McKenzie, interview, 14 April 1988.

61 Guild, interview.
62 Charles F. Phillips, 'A History of the Kroger Grocery & Baking Company', *National Marketing Review* 1, no. 3 (1936): 204–215; Kyle W. Stiegert & Vardges Hovhannisyan, 'Food Retailing in the United States: History, Trends, Perspectives', in *Structural Changes in Food Retailing: Six Country Case Studies*, ed. Kyle W. Stiegert & Dong Hwan Kim (Madison, WI: Food System Research Group, 2009), 132.
63 Bradbury, interview.
64 R. Coles, interview.
65 Merrett, 'The Making of Australia's Supermarket Duopoly,' 307.
66 McKenzie, interview, 14 April 1988.
67 Thomas, interview.
68 Emanuela Scarpellini, 'The Long Way to the Supermarket: Entrepreneurial Innovation and Adaptation in 1950s–1960s Italy', in *Transformations of Retailing in Europe after 1945*, ed. Lydia Langer & Ralph Jessen (London: Taylor and Francis: 2012), 57.
69 R. Coles, interview.
70 Matthew Bailey, 'Urban Disruption, Suburbanization and Retail Innovation: Establishing Shopping Centres in Australia', *Urban History* 47, no. 1 (2020): 155–56.
71 R. Coles, interview.
72 Merrett, 'The Making of Australia's Supermarket Duopoly', 308.
73 R. Coles, interview.
74 Seabrook, interview.
75 Stucki, interview.
76 Seabrook, interview.
77 McKenzie, interview, 14 April 1988.
78 *Ibid.*
79 Gavin J. Andrews, Robin A. Kearns, Pia Kontos and Viv Wilson, '"Their Finest Hour:" Older People, Oral Histories, and the Historical Geography of Social Life', *Social & Cultural Geography* 7, no. 2 (2006): 170.
80 J. M. Pahl and R. E. Pahl, *Managers and Their Wives: A Study of Career and Family Relationships in the Middle Class* (London: Allen Lane, 1971), 263.
81 Rob Goffee and Richard Scase, 'Organizational Change and the Corporate Career: The Restructuring of Managers' Job Aspirations', *Human Relations* 45, no. 4 (1992): 364.
82 Pahl and Pahl, *Managers and Their* Wives, 259.
83 Ely Chinoy, *Automobile Workers and the American Dream* (New York: Doubleday: 1955), 117, quoted in Colin Bell, *Middle Class Families: Social and Geographic Mobility* (London: Kegan Paul: 1968), 13.
84 North, interview, 3 October 1985.
85 Fraser, interview, 26 May 1994, Box 4749, CMA, SLV; McKenzie, interview, 31 March 1988; Mac Murton, interview by Stella Barber, 2 November 1987, Box 4766, CMA, SLV; North, interview; John Mountain, interview by Stella Barber, 19 January 1988, Box 4767, CMA, SLV.
86 Murton, interview.
87 Kanter, *Men and Women of the Corporation,* 133-36.
88 Bell, *Middle Class Families*, 14-15.
89 Goffee and Scase, 'Organizational Change', 364.

90 W. Coles, interview.
91 Harry Boyce, interview by Stella Barber, 26 October 1993, Box 4766, CMA, SLV.
92 Margaret L. Helfrich, 'The Generalized Role of the Executive's Wife', *Marriage and Family Living* 23, no. 4 (1961): 384.
93 *Ibid.*, 384–86.
94 Pahl and Pahl, *Managers and Their Wives*, 261.
95 Coulson, interview.
96 Thomas, interview.
97 Kanter, *Men and Women of the Corporation*, 110.
98 *Ibid.*, 108.
99 Mrs Schlecht in Raymond Schlecht, interview by Stella Barber, 28 June 1986, Box 4765, CMA, SLV.
100 Seabrook, interview.
101 Stucki, interview.
102 Boyce, interview.

2   Creating Continuity

Stakeholders, Narratives, and the Cadbury Brand

After revisiting her childhood memories of consuming Cadbury chocolate in rural Australia in the 1950s, Robyn Inglis was asked to reflect on the Cadbury brand and the degree to which it had changed over the following six decades. 'I don't know that it's really changed a lot', she mused, 'Probably the pieces of chocolate have got a bit smaller but [laughs] in fact, I'm sure they have. But I don't think it's really changed markedly in my memory'.[1] In response to the same question, Lucy Gransbury, who grew up in suburban Adelaide in the 1990s, replied:

> I think they [Cadbury] have rolled with the times and branched out a lot. ... I certainly think they must produce a lot more and innovative products than they did back in the day. ... So I guess they have branched out a lot more, but it's still the good old Cadbury, though.'[2]

Despite their differences in time and location, both consumers offer similar narratives of Cadbury: the brand is dynamic yet unchanged, contemporary yet timeless. In revealing the active relationship between consumers and brands, such narratives (along with the paradoxes contained therein) expose some of the fault lines that are often concealed or altogether absent from business history. More than a mere tool for locating such fissures, oral history also offers methodologies for critically engaging with them with a view to enhancing our understanding of business history.

Business history is no stranger to oral history. With its capacity to unearth and interrogate 'the complex relationships between the personal, the public and the corporate', oral history offers important insights for business historians and it is unsurprising that business historians were among the pioneers of its use.[3] While such relationships are also integral to understanding the growth and development

DOI: 10.4324/9781003171232-3

of marketing and marketing practices, marketing historians have been late coverts to oral history, only embracing it in the last decade.[4] Not surprisingly, marketing scholars focusing on contemporary issues have largely ignored oral history altogether. But with its interest in identifying the construction and conduct of broader narratives, oral history does in fact present possible applications for contemporary scholarship and practice, particularly for those interested in branding and the ways that it connected with the past.

With its focus on the present and future, the marketing industry and its attendant quest to reinvent or reinvigorate brands appear to be exemplars par excellence of Schumpeter's concept of creative destruction. However, the emergence of the heritage marketing concept presents a somewhat intriguing counterpoint. Pioneered by Mats Urde, Stephen Greyser, and John Balmer, heritage marketing underscored the importance of consistency and endurance amidst a sea of change. The past, they declared, mattered: 'A company's heritage transcends its history. A brand with a heritage has a story to tell. Heritage is and can be a vibrant part of how companies think about themselves and the values they offer their stakeholders'.[5] Seeking 'to understand better how to activate, nurture and protect heritage in the process of corporate branding', they outlined the concept of brand heritage.[6] As an aspect of a brand's identity, brand heritage lies in a brand's 'track record, longevity, core values, use of symbols and particularly in an organisational belief that its history is important'.[7] The field has since flourished. Reflecting on the concept's 'inexorable' growth, Balmer offers several reasons. He considers heritage marketing's omnitemporality to be an integral component of its appeal; insofar, it 'stressed the importance of all three timeframes; alluded to 'living history'; and underscored the significance of both change and continuity'.[8] Such features resonate with oral history methodologies and practices. While interviews are used in heritage marketing scholarship, there is no utilisation (let alone consideration) of oral history methodologies – a gap that this chapter begins to redress.

This chapter explores the relationships between brands and their stakeholders, both internal and external, using oral history interviews conducted with past and current staff (from senior managers to casuals on the factory line) and consumers of Cadbury. The interviews were undertaken as part of a commissioned history of Cadbury in Australia to celebrate the centenary of its Australian factory in Claremont, Tasmania. In addition to offering access to parts of the Cadbury story that were altogether absent from the firm's archives and the public record, the interviews offered candid and unique insights into the ways that Australians have experienced the brand over an extended period of time. Specifically, this chapter will focus on respondents' answers to the question 'has Cadbury changed as a brand'. As the opening quotes reveal, the responses to this simple question are personal, complex, and multifaceted. By unpacking these views, this chapter shows how oral history can deliver deeper insights into brands along with the narratives surrounding and underpinning them. In the process, it will also demonstrate oral history's broader value to marketing and business historians and, indeed, marketing scholars more generally.

Establishing a Presence

Cadbury's origins can be traced back to 1824 when John Cadbury opened his tea and coffee store in Birmingham.[9] It would be the business's sideline in cocoa, however, that would prove to be its making. By 1830, John Cadbury had abandoned retail to focus on manufacturing cocoa products. When the British government reduced import duties on cocoa in 1832, Cadbury was in the fortuitous position of reaching a significantly larger market than before.[10] Over the next 15 years, business boomed, compelling the firm to relocate to larger premises. Such growth also reflected the firm's astute business decisions. Where competitors' products had been inconsistently manufactured, Cadbury sought to create a point of difference by placing a stronger emphasis on quality. Their strategy was rewarded with the ultimate accolade of a royal charter in 1854. The firm's embrace of marketing ensured that the masses would be well acquainted with the Cadbury name and, indeed, its quality. Cadbury's initial store sought to stand out from the opposition from the very outset. In addition to the highly polished plate glass windows (a novelty in their own right), the firm's store used an eye-catching array of tea chests, caddies, and Chinese vases to arrest attention and generate excitement.[11] With its shift to manufacturing, the firm invested in advertising and other aspects of marketing, including distribution, ensuring that the Cadbury brand was recognisable and accessible.[12]

By the early 1850s, awareness of the Cadbury brand had extended to the Australian colonies. The first mention of the arrival of Cadbury products in the colonies occurred in South Australia in 1853.[13] Advertisements for Cadbury were also appearing in neighbouring Victoria, where the goldrush importers were able to supply a burgeoning market that included many recent arrivals who had possibly encountered the Cadbury brand in Britain.[14] Over the following decades, advertisements announcing the availability of recently arrived Cadbury products continued to appear intermittently in the press.[15] Cadbury Brothers' interest in foreign markets would grow over the 1870s, with the firm formally dispatching representatives to Ireland, Canada, Chile, and France.[16] The Australian colonies would become a part of this network in 1881 when the firm sent Thomas Elford Edwards to Melbourne. Edwards was able to build on the brand's presence and quickly built up orders for Cadbury products across Australia and New Zealand. By 1882, he was requesting additional staff from head office to assist with his increasing workload.[17] The firm also invested heavily in advertising and other promotional activities while improving its distribution operations. Business in the Australian colonies continued to grow, and by the early 1890s, Australia had become Cadbury's largest export market that was bigger than all other foreign markets combined.[18]

Cadbury's growth in Australia would be dramatically curtailed by the First World War. The British government's ban on the export of chocolate and cocoa in February 1917 combined with the Australian government's embargo on the importation of any confectioneries from other countries effectively suffocated Cadbury's Australian operations. Stocks of Cadbury products dwindled, while local chocolate and cocoa manufacturers happily took their place on the shelf. By August 1917, the firm announced that Australian stocks of its Bournville and Cadbury lines of cocoa were completely exhausted and that they did not know when the next supplies would be arriving.[19] Imports would only resume in late 1919, by which time Cadbury decided that it needed to build a local factory. The decision was also a strategic response to Australia's increased tariffs, enabling Cadbury to regain the ground that it had lost during the war and to resume its growth. It was a major investment with a significant risk, but one that would ultimately pay off – in more ways than anticipated.

Cadbury's new factory in Claremont, Tasmania, commenced chocolate production in 1922. While Claremont had been closely modelled on Cadbury's factory in Bournville, it soon became apparent that Australian conditions differed markedly to those in the UK with environmental, geographical, political, economic, and socio-cultural differences affecting almost every aspect of the firm's Australian operations. Adaptation and innovation would be integral to Cadbury's immediate and long-term success in the Australian market. While this was an understandably pragmatic response to the challenges at hand, the granting of such autonomy also set the Australian operations on a separate (though connected) trajectory from its parent company that would affect the ways that Australian staff and consumers would perceive the brand and relate to it.

Staff Loyalty

'Cadbury to me is the only brand, I guess because I worked there, because I had so much to do with it', explained Betty Stanfield, 'Yes, you went for Cadbury first, you didn't even, well I didn't even look at anything else. It was just Cadbury and that was all there was all about it'.[20] Stanfield joined Cadbury's accounts department in 1968 and would remain with the company for some 13 years. Her comments and sentiments were shared by many other interviewees who were past or current staff members. A deep connection is unsurprising for those who had spent a long time with the company and whose economic livelihood was dependent on the fortunes of the brand. While business historians have paid close attention to the contribution and impact of staff on business operations, outputs, and outcomes, the relationship between staff and brand – particularly those outside of the marketing department – has attracted less attention. Interviews conducted with staff not only illustrate how they engaged with the Cadbury brand, but also reveal the degree to which emotions have informed them and, indeed, staff recollections of them.

Loyalty to the brand was one of the key themes that emerged in staff interviews. For many, such loyalty was a logical and rational response. Those who worked at Cadbury for an extended period of time felt that their service with the firm spoke for itself. 'Well, I guess it means so much to me because I've had a big, long association with it in the family, and also eaten a lot of the product [laughs]', explained Barry Hyland, who was a second-generation Cadbury employee at Claremont.[21] Penelope Smith was another second-generation employee. While her own career with the firm in the early 1970s was relatively short, she was still grateful for what Cadbury had done for her: 'They gave me a job when I needed it so I'll buy their chocolate to keep them here'.[22]

Hyland and Smith's backgrounds (and associated connections) illustrate another key theme raised by interviewees who had a direct connection with the firm: family. References to family were not restricted to interviewees' reflections on their relationship with the brand; they were also expressed in relation to other questions both directly and indirectly. This was in part based on fact. Mark Rashleigh, who spent 32 years working in various production departments, explained the ubiquitous family references across these interviews. Families, he recalled, were a very real part of the business:

> You know, the dad might have worked at Cadbury's, and he'd put a word in for the son to go up there and because they knew the

dad, so the son would get a job up there ... there did seem to be a lot of families working up there together.[23]

Ted Best, who was the Director of the Tasmanian operations from 1976 to 1997, similarly noted the preponderance of 'second [and] third generation' staff at Claremont before offering a more pragmatic explanation for this pattern: 'Yeah, you got a bit of captive audience down here. The job mobility in Tasmania is not as great as it is in mainland states. So that's the reason we had so many employees work 40 years plus'.[24]

The significance of family ran deeper than staffing patterns. For many interviewees, the company itself was imbued with family values. 'They were a very family orientated company, very community orientated company', Rashleigh observed.[25] Intriguingly, others illustrated the same point by recounting stories that had been shared with them. Hyland, for example, told a story that had presumably been handed down to him by his father (who had commenced at Claremont in 1923):

> But it does sit in my mind where during The Depression, when so many people were out of work, that they [Cadbury] didn't ask people to leave. Because they were a family company and the interests of their employees were paramount, they asked the employees to, I think it was cut down on one day, and they could employ everyone continually without losing anyone. That was one thing that they did do during The Depression.[26]

The firm's history was similarly cited by others. Charlotte Sainsbury, whose father was the Chairman of the Australian operations from 1939 to 1953, pointed to the founding family and its religious convictions and values: 'The Quaker ethics of the Cadbury family themselves was such that they took great care of their employees'.[27] Best similarly underscored the importance of the Cadbury family as well as its active engagement with its far-flung Australian operations:

> it was a bit like a royal visit each year. You had that family sort of feeling about it, because it was still a private company at that stage, family-owned, or family and trust—family trust owned. So, it was like having your grandfather coming in, that sort of thing.[28]

Elsewhere in his interview, Best went on to situate this relationship between the Australian operations and its parent company within a broader, historical context: 'it was very much a sort of family when

I joined and Cadbury Australia was very much beholden to the UK and ... a positive interaction, but it was a sort of a parental type thing to some extent'.[29]

Expressions of pride revealed further emotional connections with Cadbury. Staff valued Cadbury's high standards in terms of product quality and the processes of manufacturing, and, indeed, identified with them. Having spent 14 years at Claremont working on the production process, John Remington was enormously proud of the work that went into chocolate production:

> I frigging [sic] loved Cadbury product, and I still do, and I love it like you wouldn't believe. It's really important to me ... even though I've tried other brands, as we all do. But I prefer Cadbury. It's just the consistency of the chocolate, the way it's made, and the ingredients that they put it into it, to me, is important.[30]

Dereck Brown spent little more than a year as a chemist at Claremont in the 1960s. Despite the brevity of his tenure, Brown echoed Remington's sentiments:

> I would have to say quality is the thing that comes to mind first and foremost. They were very, very sensitive to any imperfections that happened ... I think they were very proud of their quality and standards and that's the thing I read the most about it'.[31]

The centrality of quality in management's thinking was confirmed by Best:

> the quality systems within the company were very good and they were always progressively improving. ... the main concern at the factory level was that ... the product that you produced and delivered to the consumer was the best it possibly could be.[32]

Frank Miller started his career at Cadbury in 1977 working in organisational management. For him, it was the staff who made the brand: 'The attitude of people there was first-class, I mean, there nothing was an obstacle. It was a can-do attitude and their technical and marketing capabilities were right up there. I was proud to be part of that'.[33] The strength of this culture was noted by Doug Loveless, who commenced his career in the confectionery business at one of Cadbury's major competitors, the MacRobertson confectionery firm in Melbourne. Loveless joined Cadbury when it bought out MacRobertson in 1967.

Shortly after the takeover, Loveless was sent to Tasmania 'for a couple of weeks to be indoctrinated ... to understand the Cadbury way of life, and ... then return to our lot [in Melbourne] and duplicate the way they did business down at Claremont'. He was impressed by what he saw: 'A great culture at Claremont, wonderful, but very disciplined. A pride type discipline. They had a great pride in their work and in their product, in the way that they handled their people'.[34]

Interviewees whose family members were staff at Cadbury expressed similar sentiments. 'I was proud that my dad worked for Cadbury's and that they were helping out in our community', recalled Carole Rushbrook, who grew up on the Claremont estate that had been created for staff and their families.[35] Feelings of pride were also imbued with other emotions. Conceding that 'I'm probably a little biased', Sainsbury expressed her pride in her family's connection with Cadbury by pointing to firm's commitment to quality as well as her family's fervent and, indeed, unwavering loyalty to the brand:

> I know my mother would never have brought home chocolate from another brand. And I think, to the day my dad died, he only ever bought Cadbury chocolate because I think they were loyal and they were grateful for the sort of employer that they had. Because I didn't know it was unusual at the time, but I think, in terms of how they ran their community and their factory, it probably was quite unusual.[36]

Consistency was another attribute that staff valued. 'Beautiful, lovely smooth, rich chocolate and still is', beamed Gwen Taylor, who joined the firm's Sydney office in 1946.[37] Derreck Brown concurred, albeit in a drier tone: 'I think some product lines have ceased production and others possibly have been added. But no, I think as a product it's been remarkably consistent and remarkably sustained good quality'.[38] Others noted the consistency of the brand. Kent Wells, who had grown up next to the firm's milk processing plant at Edith Creek and also spent a summer there working as a casual, felt that Cadbury had 'remained very consistent' and that 'they haven't been involved in too many disasters that I'm aware of'.[39] While he did recall that 'there might have been something some years ago', his quick dismissal of this event as well as its impact on the brand reveals the salience of the brand image. Asked whether he felt that consumers had changed in the way that they saw the Cadbury brand, Loveless bluntly responded: 'I don't think there was any change'. This, he went to explain, was the desired response to Cadbury's efforts to build and maintain its brand image through its extensive marketing campaigns: 'You just played it [the brand image] to death'.[40]

Some interviewees, however, felt that Cadbury's much-vaunted consistency had worn away. 'I don't know that I'd have too many emotions about the place now that things have changed', explained Barry Hyland, 'People have gone. It's still very popular I believe. I don't think the product's as good as it used to be'.[41] Charlotte Sainsbury was saddened by the changes that she had seen since her father headed Claremont:

> the ethos of the company changed from the time it was taken over. And that is a disappointment – seeing the housing estate sold off and the benefits that the workers had reduced. I just felt that the people working there weren't as valued as they had been in the past.

However, Sainsbury felt that the product itself had remained true: 'I think the chocolate and the quality of the chocolate ... probably remained the same'.[42]

The split between perceptions and reality was perhaps most evident in the interviews with staff who had worked in Cadbury's marketing department. Rod Heath had joined the business in 1995 as a brand manager of bars. An unrepentant chocoholic, he was passionate about the Cadbury brand and its products: 'I love chocolate, I did before I joined the firm ... I lived on it, I'd miss lunches often and I'd just eat it all the time. And people said to me 'how come you're just not obese?'. While he conceded that he was not underweight, he nevertheless felt that there was some truth in the firm's marketing spiel that claimed that Cadbury chocolate was 'born of a plant food'. However, Heath's position also gave an insight into the actual product and, indeed, its relationship with the brand:

> I lifted the veil a bit because I had the privilege of knowing that there were for Cadbury Dairy Milk it's a variable recipe anyway depending on where the cows are grazing and the cooking processes that are in various factories. ... It is a bit of a mirage that you think over time that you're so loyal to this beautiful chocolate yet underneath the actual recipe is continually being altered, changed, concessions are made.[43]

Tim Stanford was a contemporary of Heath's in the marketing department in the late 1990s and early 2000s. He was proud of the brand and the fact that during his time, it had been voted as one of Australia's most trusted brands. But in recent years, he felt that Cadbury had undone this good work by reducing their product sizes. As a marketer who had worked closely with the brand, Stanford understood that this simple cost-cutting measure went against the values and emotions that interviewees associated with the Cadbury brand:

> It's not so trusted now because consumers are incredibly conscious of Freddo Frogs getting smaller and smaller and smaller ... they [Cadbury] would have lost some of that trust and lost some of that probably human personable side. They would have lost a bit of the personality fabric. It's probably seen more as a corporation now rather than a company run by Australians for Australians.[44]

While Cadbury's softening share of the Australian market in recent years indicated that there was some truth to these claims, such concerns nevertheless stand out more for illustrating the depth of the emotional investment that staff had made in the Cadbury brand. And, as such, they ought to be subjected to closer scrutiny.

An Individual yet Collective Experience

The concerns that Cadbury's recent actions had tarnished its brand image by bringing consumers face to face with the stark realities of business contained an implicit assumption that consumers had a fickle relationship with the brand. Interviewees presented a different story. Musing on the relationship that she had developed with the Cadbury brand, Sonja Grdosic's explanation displayed a greater level of depth and, indeed, resilience:

> It's a brand and ... I think as I've got older ... I've realised there are other brands of chocolate but somehow I always go back to Cadbury's, always insisting on Cadbury's. So, there must be some emotional type of loyalty there, loyalty with the brand. And I have tried the others, the more upmarket brands but it's almost as if you're sort of so comfortable always going back to Cadbury.[45]

Grdosic was not alone in her views – similar comments and sentiments were expressed by many interviewees. Like staff members, consumers' connections with Cadbury were also deeply emotional, drawing on personal experiences, memories, and sentiments. However, as Stefan Schwarzkopf bemusedly notes, such stories and experiences have been largely overlooked by marketing (and business) historians: 'While customer-centric marketing theory asserts that the consumer is the alpha and omega of all marketing activities, and increasingly the initiator of marketing innovations, most marketing historical research does not seem to see it that way'.[46] By speaking to consumers, oral history not only helps to address this obvious deficiency, but also creates a more holistic perspective of brands and the ways they function. To this end, the interviews conducted with Cadbury consumers demonstrate that they are actively engaging with the brand and that their emotional connections with Cadbury are informed within a series of different personal and collective contexts.

For consumers, the relationship with Cadbury was premised on the product itself. Taste was integral to this experience. 'We've had the other brands', confessed Graham Elphick, 'but their squares are so much smaller and they have more of a bitter taste than the Cadburys. The Cadburys has a nice sweet, smoothing, relaxing, feel good taste'.[47] Elphick would go on to explain how the taste was also part of a broader experience that took him back to his childhood:

> Yes, yes, every time we went to the theatre because, the good thing about it, right, you could sit there and, as my father always said, put the chocolate on the top of your tongue, don't bite it, suck it. And you'd sit there in the back of the theatre off in another world and this beautiful smooth, soothing taste of the old Cadburys, it used to make you feel good. I don't know what was in it, but it always made you feel good. It still does.[48]

Taste evoked equally strong memories for others too. Robert Brown instantaneously recalled the flavour of Cadbury chocolate even though he was no longer in a position to consume it: 'My mouth starts to water. But the only thing now, I've had a bit of bowel problem. Bowel cancer. And I'm not allowed to eat chocolate'.[49] While changing tastes was noted by several older consumers, they nevertheless pointed out that they had not abandoned Cadbury. 'Yes, these days I really like the dark chocolates peppermint cream, the Old Gold [a Cadbury line] peppermint cream. That's my favourite today', declared Margaret Wilmot, while Wendy Gordon noted, 'I do prefer a dark chocolate now. I find they're not as sweet as the milk chocolate but every now and then I will buy a milk one just for a change'.[50]

Discussions of Cadbury's taste prompted further reflection on the connections between product and brand. Like staff, consumers considered consistency to be an integral part of the Cadbury brand and its appeal. 'Strangely, I think it's been very consistent, it hasn't changed a lot at all, no. The colours, the appearance of the promotions. No, it hasn't, in my mind it hasn't anyhow', reflected Dennis Tedman.[51] Such sentiments were echoed by Elizabeth Ruthven: 'Well it [Cadbury as a brand] means a lot. I think consistency and reliability. Yes, what they say is what they deliver and the taste usually stayed the same. I don't think there was too much experimenting of taste'.[52] Consistency thus provided comfort, stability, and, indeed, an emotional connection with one's own past.

Personal memories were deeply intwined with ideas of family. Where staff interviews discussed real and imagined families, consumer stories very much focused on their own families and their collective experiences. 'I've always had a sweet tooth and so has the rest of our family', explained Susan Black. She vividly recalled how 'My Mum used to love the fruit and nut and Dad really liked the Caramello. He didn't have the best teeth so he couldn't eat the nut [laughs]'.[53] Robyn Inglis identified her mother tastes and the impact it had on her family:

> Cadbury as a brand was something I grew up with. As I recall back when I was a child, there were two probably main brands of chocolates. And that was Cadbury and then perhaps Nestlé ... I'm sure there were a couple of others, but in our family, it was Cadburys all the way. It was my mother's favourite and she always had the fruit and nut variety or the plain milk chocolate hidden away in the cupboard that we sometimes were able to have a nibble of.[54]

Carol Black similarly underscored the importance of family, noting that she and her sister had remained true to the brand since their childhood in the 1950s: 'I think always it's still a family ... it's probably a hangover from our youth that we just enjoy Cadbury's Dairy Milk or the ones with nuts in and things like that, you know?'.[55]

Such memories understandably display a strong connection with the interviewee's own childhood. Intriguingly, various interviewees went to explain how these experiences and memories continued to inform their consumption practices. 'Yeah, and it was just something that we loved and growing up, yeah, we just kept eating it [laughs]', noted Susan Black.[56] Carol Black recounted a similar experience, but also reveals the way in which her past has affected her own children's consumption patterns: 'Yeah, it's just it's always been a family favourite. In our family, anyway, so, and, to my mind, it still is. I mean, even my children, they always like Cadbury's, yes. So, [laughs], it's been carried on'.[57]

Consumer relationships with Cadbury were also informed by broader ideas of kinship and connection. Many noted the importance of the fact that Cadbury products were manufactured locally. Tasmanians were particularly proud of 'their' Claremont factory. '[T]he Cadburys name to me is synonymous with Hobart. And it was just a landmark as far as I was concerned', observed David Stubbs.[58] Carole Rushbrook noted that Tasmanians' relationship with Cadbury was also informed by economics: 'I think, in terms ... of Tasmania, that it was, the factory is here and we need to support this'.[59] The importance of the Claremont plant for locals was not lost on mainlanders like Dennis Tedman:

> It also gives an image of something that is well established and a part of Tasmanian culture almost, it's part of being Tasmanian. The factory seems to be there forever and the locals regard it as theirs and, I know it's probably owned by other people, but it is regarded as a Tasmanian feature.[60]

For consumers living on the mainland, Cadbury was equally an Australian brand. Margaret Summers, who grew up in 1960s Melbourne, thus explained that 'I always used to think Cadbury was Australian because of the factory they had in Claremont in Tassie'.[61] Growing up nearby Cadbury's Ringwood plant in suburban Melbourne in the 1970s and 1980s, Dave O'Neil did not necessarily see it as Tasmanian brand: 'Oh, Cadbury is like a very solid Australian—well, I thought it was Australian, but obviously it's an English chocolate brand—a purple brand that we grew up with'.[62] Many interviewees relayed a similar story, confessing that they had only recently learned that Cadbury was not an Australian-owned firm. However, this realisation did not necessarily change their views of the brand or, indeed, their emotional connection with it. Dennis Tedman, for example, mused:

> It seems to be, in my mind, a part of being Australian, the Cadbury's chocolate bit. Nestlé and other brands have never really reached that prominence in my mind and, yeah, so it seems to be ... I know it's not owned by Australia anymore, but it has a feel about being an Australian identifier.[63]

Despite growing up some twenty years later, Sonja Grdosic similarly maintained the idea that Cadbury was a local firm even though she knew that it was not: 'It's a brand that Australians have seen on the supermarket shelves and it's sort of like, it's so Australian but we know it's not, isn't it. [Laughs] I thought it was owned by Kraft or something'.[64]

Consumer responses reveal the impact of Cadbury's long-term commitment to marketing. Operating as a direct link between consumers and the brands, marketing played a key role in both enhancing Cadbury's visibility and, indeed, eliciting the desired consumer emotional responses to the brand. The firm's marketing activities incorporated multiple formats to reach the consumer. Interviewees' memories noted three distinct (yet highly integrated) aspects of Cadbury's marketing – in store presence, advertising, and packaging.

When discussing their preference for Cadbury products over other brands, interviewees ruminated on the reasons why Cadbury was the leader in the marketplace. Not surprisingly, taste was cited as an important reason for choosing Cadbury chocolate. However, interviewees also noted that their capacity to choose was in fact limited. Margaret Summers thus compared the situation in her youth to what she had experienced in more recent times:

> I doubt whether there was that many different brands on the market then. Darrell Lea used to sell only in their own shops. I'm pretty sure they weren't available in milk bars [corner stores] in those times. And it might have been Nestlé from memory.[65]

Margaret Wilmott echoed this account. Noting that 'there was Mac-Robertsons in the early days but they were very small so the competition was really only Nestlé back then', Willmott observed that Cadbury has 'a lot more competition these days'.[66] With so few competitors, Cadbury was able to use its size to dominate shelf space in stores, which, in turn, helped ensure that it would dominate sales.

Visuals were another key part of Cadbury's merchandising efforts. The brand's distinctive colour scheme was regularly noted by consumers. 'I remember lots of different types of chocolate', recalled Trevor Smart, 'but Cadbury were the ones that stood out because of the probably the wrapper. The purple wrapper'.[67] Pauline Dine similarly mused: 'I guess it's the colours that stand out in the brand initially; the beautiful deep purple colours'.[68] For Margaret Summers, the significance of the colour ran deep: 'that purpley-blue was always associated with Cadbury brand. They very obviously kept a close guard on the copyrights of that colour and so you knew straight away what you were getting'.[69] Although Summers' account underscores the deep connection between the colour and the brand, it also illustrates how longer-term memories could be informed by more recent developments. The colour purple was only connected with the Dairy Milk line of chocolate, not the Cadbury brand as a whole. A more formal effort to connect Cadbury with the colour purple only took place in the late 1990s and early 2000s when the firm launched a series of court cases in Australia and elsewhere to grant it exclusive rights of a particular purple tone (Pantone 2685).[70] While such details certainly illustrate the fallible nature of memories, the emotional attachment with the colour was nevertheless deep-seated and genuine.

Cadbury's in-store presence and packaging strategies were under-pinned by its broader advertising efforts. Advertising in media outlets sought to establish a broader awareness of the brand and its lines, and, in turn, to create and inform the emotional connection between con-sumers and the brand. A major in the nineteenth century, Cadbury continued to invest heavily in the twentieth century. Recalling his childhood some 60 years earlier, Graham Elphick readily recounted the impact of Cadbury's advertising:

> Cadbury, to me, are pretty much an icon because I remember from a very early age as a young kid, and I was born in the war years and food was rationed. But gradually, when they came out from the rationing, we all suddenly discovered Cadburys. Everywhere we went they used to have advertising. I can remember the adver-tising, there was a glass and a half in each block and I loved the young boy who sang the block of Cadbury's chocolate. And that always stuck in my mind ...[71]

Cadbury's 'Glass and a half' featured prominently in the memories of several interviewees. Reflecting on the promotional materials that she encountered when growing up in the 1950s, Elizabeth Ruthven instantly recalled the slogan and its centrality: 'the Cadbury Dairy Milk symbol has always been there and I'm pretty sure that any signs featured that more than anything, the glass and a half and the pouring of the mild into the block. And that was the main thing'.[72]

Growing up four decades later, Lucy Gransbury similarly recalled the slogan: 'immediately I picture their branding, the purple and the half glass, but—glass and a half—but I think, I really see Cadbury as having a sense of fun'.[73] While Gransbury initially misquotes the slogan, her immediate and automatic self-correction underscores the degree to which it had permeated the consumer mindset. For some respondents, recounting the famous 'glass and a half' slogan prompted them to think a little more about its origins as well as its relevance. 'God, that's a memory. The glass and a half', reflected Dave O'Neil,

'Because that's what, I suppose they were trying to get the parents in, weren't they? They were trying to get the mums in with their claims of a glass and half of milk'.[74] Robert Brown was motivated to question the veracity of the claim in light of the recent reduction in size of the Cadbury's blocks. Brown thus recounted how he had recently spoken to a Cadbury's representative at his local supermarket:

> And I said, 'Those little ones. How do you get a glass and a half in those little ones?' [Laughs] And he said, 'That's just thing.' He says. 'There's always a glass and half in the mix.' He said, 'There mightn't be a glass and half in the little one, but it's in the chocolate itself. They just move it and put it in different moulds ... but there's a glass and half in every one.' So, I couldn't argue with that.[75]

The veracity of the famous Cadbury slogan was not the only part of the brand to be questioned. Although interviewees happily relayed their deep and profoundly fond memories of Cadbury, some observed that their relationship had changed – something that interviews with staff in the marketing department had highlighted when discussing the shrinking sizes of chocolate blocks. However, size reductions did not appear to be a major issue for interviewees. The only interviewee to reference this issue directly was Lucy Gransbury, who dismissed it:

> I don't know that it's [the Cadbury brand] really changed a lot. Probably the pieces of chocolate have got a bit smaller but [laughs] in fact, I'm sure they have. But I don't think it's really changed markedly in my memory.[76]

Dorothy Edwards, who had grown up eating Cadbury in the 1950s, identified a different problem. But like Gransbury, she did not necessarily feel that it had diminished her love for the brand:

> DOROTHY EDWARDS: It's a little bit different now I think but I still like it.
> INTERVIEWER: In what way is it a little bit different?
> DOROTHY EDWARDS: Well, as I said before, the Cadbury box of chocolates, all the flavours have gone solid where they used to be like a runny, creamy, and I was used to that. I loved that but now ... And Snack, Snack used to have like caramel flavours. Now they're all set, do you know what I'm saying?[77]

Other interviewees, however, were less circumspect about the changes and the impact they had on their relationship with the Cadbury brand.

They expressed disappointment that the brand had not remained true to its past. Pauline Dine thus lamented: 'So it's a shame that ... Cadbury's had lost a lot of the atmosphere and meaning of the brand a bit, the family memory of the brand and the chocolate and all that went around it, yes'.[78] Rocelyn Ives shared a similar view but offered a more detailed explanation of how the Cadbury brand had changed in recent times:

> I think it has [changed]. There's the big slip-up for me was when they changed that recipe which is in more recent times and the expansion – OK, that it was not particularly belonging anywhere anymore. It was a global community. Cadbury's is now a global community. But when they changed that recipe and Cadbury's was no longer the chocolate that it used to be I think it lost a lot of its kudos, you know what I mean? It lost a lot of its shine because once it always was the chocolate that everyone went to. Cadbury's was 'the chocolate', you know what I mean [laughs].[79]

Carole Rushbrook concurred. The impact of such shifts, coupled with the broader changes to the market (such as increased competition), prompted a re-evaluation of her relationship with the brand that had occupied an important place in her youth: 'I think, as a brand, I don't see that I need to be quite so loyal to Cadbury's these days'.[80] While hardly condemning, such comments nevertheless confirmed the fear expressed by staff interviewees – that the Cadbury brand was perceived to be drifting away from its historical moorings.

*** *** ***

From the 1980s, businesses have increasingly recognised the importance of brands as intangible assets and have duly developed different methodologies to determine their value. While a brand's heritage is but a single factor in such calculations, it is nevertheless an important one – especially where a brand can lay claim to a long and proud history. In order to understand the significance of this history in any accurate or, indeed, meaningful way, we therefore need to be able to unpack it. As this chapter has shown, oral history offers a unique tool for undertaking this task. Interviewee comments and insights concerning the Cadbury brand not only provided details that are absent from formal and written records, but also functioned as important documents in their own right. By collecting and analysing these narratives, our use of oral history enabled us to identify core aspects of the Cadbury brand and its heritage, as well as their meaning and significance to brand stakeholders. Such narratives were shown to be complex and multilayered, informed by a series of interactions over an extended period of time.

Interviews with internal and external stakeholders provided an opportunity to dig deeper into the brand and to unearth the small but important differences in the ways that these different groups viewed it. Staff interviewees were understandably informed by direct experience with Cadbury as an employer. However, the firm's support of its workers was only a part of the broader narrative being conveyed. Cadbury's commitment to its product was equally important. Such experiences led staff to associate the brand with ideas of loyalty, family, and consistency. While external stakeholders expressed similar views, their outlook was informed by a different set of experiences. Consumers' major direct interaction with the brand was via consumption. Indirect experiences, however, would play a more important role in informing their outlooks. Childhood and family memories loomed large. These were also connected to marketing and advertising, which played (and continued to play) a key role in connecting consumers to the brand and, indeed, informing their interpretations of it. The consistencies between internal and external stakeholder accounts attest to the strength of the Cadbury brand, but also help account for its longevity in the Australian market. Such consistencies additionally point to the limitations of Schumpeter's creative destruction thesis for business historians – efforts to establish, maintain, or enhance constancy also play an important role in business history.

The interviewees' comments on Cadbury's perceived drift from its heritage further attest to the usefulness of oral history for business historians. While the identification of challenges threatening or undermining the Cadbury brand provides further insights into marketing practices, the broader lesson concerns the methodological approach itself. By asking researchers to consider the structure and format of the narratives being told, where they come from, and what they reveal about the different stakeholders that recount them, oral history methodologies enable us to access and, indeed, better understand those intangible aspects of business history.

Notes

1 Robyn Inglis, interview by Robert Crawford, 12 October 2020, Mondelēz Australia Heritage Collection.
2 Lucy Gransbury, interview by Robert Crawford, 16 February 2021, Mondelēz Australia Heritage Collection.

3 Rob Perks, 'Corporations are People Too!: Business and Corporate Oral History in Britain', *Oral History* 38, no. 1, (Spring 2010): 49.
4 Robert Crawford and Matthew Bailey, 'Speaking of Research: Oral History and Marketing History', *Journal of Historical Research in Marketing* 10, no. 1 (2017): 109.
5 Mats Urde, Stephen Greyser, & John Balmer, 'Corporate Brands with a Heritage', *Journal of Brand Management* 15, no. 1 (2007): 17.
6 *Ibid.*, 4.
7 *Ibid.*, 4–5.
8 John Balmer, 'Introduction to Corporate Heritage', in *Foundations of Corporate Heritage*, ed. John Balmer (Abingdon: Routledge, 2017), 3.
9 Cited in Iolo A. Williams, *The Firm of Cadbury* (London: Constable and Co., 1931), 5.
10 John Bradley, *Cadbury's Purple Reign: The Story Behind Chocolate's Best-loved Brand* (Chichester: John Wiley & Sons, 2008), 4–6.
11 Carl Chinn, *The Cadbury Story: A Short History* (Studley, Warwickshire: Brewin Books, 2018), 4.
12 Chinn, *The Cadbury Story*, 14.
13 'Second Day's Sale Friday', *South Australian Register*, 8 February 1853, 1.
14 'Cadbury's', *Argus*, 30 June 1854, 1.
15 'J&J. Burns', *Telegraph*, 19 November 1874, 4; 'Imports', *Sydney Morning Herald*, 22 January 1878, 4; 'Shipping', *Cornwall Chronicle*, 1 February 1879, 2.
16 Williams, *The Firm of Cadbury*, 45.
17 Obituary. T. E. Edwards, *Bournville Works Magazine*, February 1926, 62.
18 'Export Summary 1894', 1894, Cadbury Brothers, Limited in Australia: Trading Accounts and Balance Sheets, Cadbury Archive – Mondelēz International, Claremont, Australia.
19 'Groceries', *Newcastle Morning Herald and Miners' Advocate*, 4 August 1917, 9.
20 Betty Stanfield, interview by Robert Crawford, 23 September 2020, Mondelēz Australia Heritage Collection.
21 Barry Hyland, interview by Robert Crawford, 18 September 2020, Mondelēz Australia Heritage Collection.
22 Penelope Smith, interview by Robert Crawford, 22 September 2020, Mondelēz Australia Heritage Collection.
23 Mark Rashleigh, interview by Robert Crawford, 29 October 2020, Mondelēz Australia Heritage Collection.
24 Ted Best, interview by Robert Crawford, 10 November 2020, Mondelēz Australia Heritage Collection.
25 Mark Rashleigh, interview by Robert Crawford, 29 October 2020, Mondelēz Australia Heritage Collection.
26 Hyland, interview.
27 Charlotte Sainsbury, interview by Robert Crawford, 14 September 2020, Mondelēz Australia Heritage Collection.
28 Best, interview.
29 *Ibid.*
30 John Remington, interview by Robert Crawford, 16 September 2020, Mondelēz Australia Heritage Collection.

31 Derreck Brown, interview by Robert Crawford, 15 October 2020, Mondelēz Australia Heritage Collection.
32 Best, interview.
33 Frank Miller, interview by Robert Crawford, 9 February 2021, Mondelēz Australia Heritage Collection.
34 Doug Loveless, interview by Robert Crawford, 17 December 2020, Mondelēz Australia Heritage Collection.
35 Carole Rushbrook, interview by Robert Crawford, 8 December 2020, Mondelēz Australia Heritage Collection.
36 Sainsbury, interview.
37 Gwen Taylor, interview by Robert Crawford, 28 September 2020, Mondelēz Australia Heritage Collection.
38 D. Brown, interview.
39 Kent Wells, interview by Robert Crawford, 9 September 2020, Mondelēz Australia Heritage Collection.
40 Loveless, interview.
41 Hyland, interview.
42 Sainsbury, interview.
43 Rod Heath, interview by Robert Crawford, 24 September 2020, Mondelēz Australia Heritage Collection.
44 Tim Stanford, interview by Robert Crawford, 13 September 2020, Mondelēz Australia Heritage Collection.
45 Sonja Grdosic, interview by Robert Crawford, 3 September 2020, Mondelēz Australia Heritage Collection.
46 Stefan Schwarzkopf, 'Marketing History from Below: Towards a Paradigm Shift in Marketing Historical Research', *Journal of Historical Research in Marketing* 7, no. 3 (2015): 296.
47 Graham Elphick, interview by Robert Crawford, 22 September 2020, Mondelēz Australia Heritage Collection.
48 Ibid.
49 Robert Brown, interview by Robert Crawford, 23 October 2020, Mondelēz Australia Heritage Collection.
50 Margaret Wilmott, interview by Robert Crawford, 11 September 2020, Mondelēz Australia Heritage Collection; Wendy Gordon, interview by Robert Crawford, 2 October 2020, Mondelēz Australia Heritage Collection.
51 Dennis Tedman, interview by Robert Crawford, 21 September 2020, Mondelēz Australia Heritage Collection.
52 Elizabeth Ruthven, interview by Robert Crawford, 25 September 2020, Mondelēz Australia Heritage Collection.
53 Susan Black, interview by Robert Crawford, 3 September 2020, Mondelēz Australia Heritage Collection.
54 Robyn Inglis, interview by Robert Crawford, 12 October 2020, Mondelēz Australia Heritage Collection.
55 Carol Black, interview by Robert Crawford, 27 January 2021, Mondelēz Australia Heritage Collection.
56 S. Black, interview.
57 C. Black, interview.
58 David Stubbs, interview by Robert Crawford, 23 October 2020, Mondelēz Australia Heritage Collection.

59 Rushbrook, interview.
60 Dennis Tedman, interview by Robert Crawford, 21 September 2020, Mondelēz Australia Heritage Collection.
61 Margaret Summers, interview by Robert Crawford, 4 September 2020, Mondelēz Australia Heritage Collection.
62 Dave O'Neil, interview by Robert Crawford, 19 February 2021, Mondelēz Australia Heritage Collection.
63 Tedman, interview.
64 Grdosic, interview.
65 Summers, interview.
66 Wilmott, interview.
67 Trevor Smart, interview by Robert Crawford, 4 November 2020, Mondelēz Australia Heritage Collection.
68 Pauline Dine, interview by Robert Crawford, 1 September 2020, Mondelēz Australia Heritage Collection.
69 Summers, interview.
70 Robert Crawford, *More than a Glass and a Half: A History of Cadbury in Australia* (Canberra: Halstead, 2022), 130.
71 Elphick, interview.
72 Elizabeth Ruthven, interview by Robert Crawford, 25 September 2020, Mondelēz Australia Heritage Collection.
73 Lucy Gransbury, interview by Robert Crawford, 16 February 2021, Mondelēz Australia Heritage Collection.
74 O'Neil, interview.
75 R. Brown, interview.
76 Gransbury, interview.
77 Dorothy Edwards, interview by Robert Crawford, 1 October 2020, Mondelēz Australia Heritage Collection.
78 Pauline Dine, interview by Robert Crawford, 1 September 2020, Mondelēz Australia Heritage Collection.
79 Rocelyn Ives, interview by Robert Crawford, 10 September 2020, Mondelēz Australia Heritage Collection.
80 Rushbrook, interview.

3 Spatial Continuity

Retail 'Town Halls' in Post-War Australia

Lend Lease was one of the most important shopping centre developers in Australia during the second half of the twentieth century. In an interview reflecting on his own career and changes in the industry, former CEO of Lend Lease Development, Richard Clarke, recalled:

> my beacon on the hill was to try and extract as much value from the shopping centre as possible. And that did not mean the narrow definition of just screwing up the rent. That was a meaningless exercise, counterproductive in the long run because you can only get so much rent out of any different tenant before they go off the edge of the cliff ... We were finding a lot of value was created by better rentals being achieved in the new shops, because they were whiz-bang, they looked good, the tenants tended to be more professional ... by redeveloping and remixing it with good tenants who were more professional, you get a higher rent ... and the leverage is enormous.[1]

Clarke's protégé, Michael Lloyd, also told a story of adaptation, but couched it in terms of meeting the needs of local communities:

> all we're doing is managing these community spaces which are an integral part of the built environment ... If you take an outer suburb that's been ... created recently, they've got no heart. They've got no soul. They've got no town square. The shopping centre became the town square.[2]

This chapter draws on oral history interviews with 22 Australian retail property executives who were recruited using a snowball recruitment methodology. The themes of increasing professionalism, continual adaptation, and the creation of community spaces, mentioned by both

DOI: 10.4324/9781003171232-4

Clarke and Lloyd, run through many of these interviews. These themes form a narrative that both explains and justifies the rapid growth, stability, and success of shopping centres in Australia. In essence, this story suggests that while retailers were subject to the forces of creative destruction, the shopping centres that housed them proved immune to its effects. In this historical account, astute retail property entrepreneurs and executives leveraged the gale of disruption that transformed retailing in the second half of the twentieth century to add value to their pre-planned shopping environments. They succeeded because the shopping centre format proved flexible enough to continually incorporate new retail models, while the industry itself was able to constantly update and improve its practices. One aspect of this was the refinement of market research which was deployed to shape developments more strategically to their surrounding trade areas. This enabled shopping centres to become essential hubs in the urban landscape and, according to several executives, form a new type of 'town square'.

Renato Rosaldo argues that 'doing oral history involves telling stories about stories people tell about themselves'.[3] In the case of business history, these stories are partly about the interviewees themselves, and partly about the firms and industries within which they have worked. As with all oral histories, each interview in this project relied upon the act of remembering, raising a range of questions about what is remembered, why it is remembered, and how authentic that memory might be.[4] Being attendant to these questions moves our 'focus from whether narratives are true or false to narratives' origins and effects'.[5] In this instance, the stories told by retail property executives provide valuable information about how the industry changed over time and why it was able to harness creative destruction. However, listening to the interviews 'against the grain' also allows us to interrogate how the industry understands and presents itself.[6]

As Zundel et al. note, history and identity are closely interlinked and are bound together by narratives.[7] When used strategically, historical narratives can be resources for organisations, and in this case, an entire industry.[8] Oral histories with retail property executives reveal a service mythology, in which the growth and success of shopping centres was a direct result of meeting the needs of shoppers and communities. This mythology serves a legitimising role for an industry that in the 1980s was accused of monopolising retail geographies and using its position of dominance to inhibit market forces and exploit specialty retail tenants. This oral history project, then, helps articulate the distinctive features and enduring characteristics of the Australian retail property industry, while also revealing the strategic benefits of a shared industry narrative claiming that shopping centres have evolved to serve local communities.

Australian Shopping Centre Development

Large pre-planned shopping centres were launched in Australia in the late 1950s. They were built in response to increasing levels of car ownership, the mass internal migration of Australian citizens to suburban areas, and an economic boom.[9] They helped overturn city-centric retail hierarchies that had developed in response to mass public transport since the late nineteenth century. Australians visited the United States to gain retail property know-how and drew on American models when designing and building shopping centres. They also borrowed the tripartite definition of regional, community, and neighbourhood centres that was used in America.[10] This indicated the relative size of trade areas, parking facilities, and anchor stores. Department stores anchored regional centres. Supermarkets anchored convenience-oriented neighbourhood centres.[11] Shopping centres offered comfortable, safe, and air-conditioned shopping environments with convenient car parking.[12] While not all early centres were immediately successful, the format quickly gained acceptance in the Australian market.[13]

The retail property industry did not exist in Australia in the mid-1950s. Shopping centre construction quickly became the most dynamic area of retail development in the country.[14] Australia's early centres often included open air sections and tended to be dominated by their anchor stores, which could occupy as much as half of their floor space. Entrepreneurs were active early developers, and by the 1970s began replacing retailers as the most important builders of shopping centres. By 1969, Australia had 79 neighbourhood, 25 community, and 28 regional shopping centres, which were now usually designed as fully enclosed retail environments.[15] As more and more were built, complaints emerged that shopping centres held geographic monopolies over retail space, because they had rendered obsolete traditional high streets which were struggling to survive.[16]

By 1995, there were 659 neighbourhood, 174 community (or sub-regional), and 65 regional shopping centres in Australia. These all contained far more shops than earlier iterations of the three shopping centre types.[17] As new retail brands or formats arrived in Australia across this period, shopping centres proved capable of absorbing them, improving their own value and magnetism in the process. Many of these formats, such as supermarkets, discount department stores (DDSs), and category killers, were highly disruptive to other retailers.[18] The shopping centre proved sustainable because it could offer these disruptive retailers the locational advantages of well-designed, concentrated retail environments with car parking in strong catchment zones. As these retail formats moved into shopping centres, older formats like variety stores and small-scale department stores lost competitiveness and were replaced.

Industry Professionalisation

As development boomed during the 1970s and 1980s, however, it became apparent that the industry was suffering from a shortage of expertise. This produced a range of pressures, including adversarial relationships with tenants and criticisms that poor practices within the industry were inhibiting the free operation of the retail market.[19] Specialty tenants and their retail trade organisations began agitating for government protections from what they described as rapacious landlords.[20] Many of these retailers were inexperienced and mis-aligned with the increasingly corporatised shopping centre environment. Richard Clarke described them as 'mum-and-dad' retailers. These were people who moved into retailing with little background, who lacked any professional marketing expertise, and who fitted out their stores in a rudimentary fashion. As a result, they failed to generate the sales of more professional operators. For landlords, this meant lower rental returns and, consequently, lower capital valuations of their assets.[21]

Industry rhetoric at the time tended to blame retailers for under-performing,[22] but there was also an acknowledgement that rapid growth had produced problems within retail property firms themselves, including 'cowboy' managers who played fast and loose with the rules.[23] Specialty retailers complained that key money or bribes were being extracted by some leasing executives in exchange for shopping centre tenancies.[24] And they argued that significant power differentials between landlords and tenants resulted in poor treatment and steep rent hikes.[25] Faced with the threat of government intervention over what was being portrayed as unconscionable conduct, the industry needed to self-regulate. Westfield Leasing Executive, Ian Newton, acknowledged that

> the shopping centre industry prior to 1984 was a little bit dicey in terms of people taking secret commissions. ... I'm not saying I know this or anyone who did it, but this is what we understood was going on.'[26]

Newton, however, went on to give an example of bribes being initiated, not by retail property executives, but by retailers. He recounts a story in which a retailer, attempting to secure a shopping centre lease, placed an envelope containing cash into a colleague's handbag. 'Embarrassed and humiliated', she ejected the retailer from her office and cancelled his proposed tenancy.[27]

The more serious issue that threatened to bring down regulatory controls on the industry, however, was the question of whether retail property managers were exploiting their positions to take advantage of small retail operators.[28] Newton was recruited from Lend Lease to Westfield in 1984. He recalls that there were 'many stories' circulating in the industry about inappropriate or even illegal behaviour as part of 'a culture that had been acknowledged but not dealt with'. In a meeting at the end of his application process with Westfield, when he was offered the role of National Director of Leasing, Newton says that Frank Lowy, co-founder of Westfield, described tenant exploitation as an 'impediment' to business. Lowy reportedly told him: 'if there's ever been anything untoward in the leasing area … going forward, it's not acceptable. You are to be ruthless in policing this... You must stamp anything out that has the potential to sully our name'.[29]

Poor practice had become a liability.[30] By the 1980s, the shopping centre form held widespread public acceptance. Retailers recognised it as the controlling power in retail geographies. The biggest developers were public companies. Large institutional investors were involved in ownership structures. Power could be wielded far more effectively through legal channels. The industry as a whole sought to reform its public image, remove aberrant behaviour, and standardise management practices through training schemes aimed at professionalising conduct.[31] This was not enough to ward off government legislation, which was applied to retail tenancies in all Australian states from the mid-1980s onwards.[32] But it was an important moment in the industry's history that introduced formal structures of accountability within firms, and standardised benchmarks for managerial behaviour and performance.

The need to improve management was also evident in other areas. The leasing of space to inefficient 'mum-and-dad' retailers, for example, became unacceptable as the scale and financial complexity of developments increased. Richard Clarke's firm, Lend Lease, was an industry leader in the push to professionalise its executive ranks. Clarke, who held a university engineering qualification, moved from the development division of Lend Lease to the retail division in 1980. Accustomed to working with graduates or postgraduate engineers and architects, he noticed a distinct difference in workplace culture and employee capabilities. He recalled that

> the guys who were managing the centres were guys who had come up through the ranks of salesmen of some sort... their vision was fairly narrow... I would say about 90 percent of them were not of the calibre that we required.[33]

Market Research

The evolution of marketing within Lend Lease provides a good example of the changes that Clarke and others pursued. Michael Lloyd who worked for Clarke and eventually led the Lend Lease retail division recalls that marketing managers in even the biggest retail property firms 'were all quasi-entertainers'. Many had career backgrounds in radio. Some had worked as the master of ceremonies on cruise ships. Their shopping centre roles, Lloyd claimed, did not involve 'marketing in terms of marketing-being-the-exercise-involved-in-the-changing-of-the-product-to-suit-the-needs-of-the-consumer'.[34] Rather, they organised promotions such as appearances from television personalities or music stars on stages in shopping centre central courts. There were also promotional competitions designed to draw crowds. Lloyd claimed that:

> Lend Lease had the one that was tops of anything: bed making competitions. People came from miles around ... and these people could make a bed in like three seconds. These women had these things and they had to fold their own sheets that they had to put on the bed. Um, two sheets, a blanket, an eiderdown, and a pillowcase on the pillow. And they could get everything ready, and they'd pick it up and go whoosh ... And they'd get around and in five seconds they'd made the bloody bed. Then you get to the state championships and the national championships. This was the biggest bloody thing in the world: the Australian bed making competitions.[35]

Ian Newton and Westfield General Manager, Alan Briggs, offered similar accounts. Newton noted that 'we had what we would call promotion managers, who'd have the fattest lady in the world come in; the tallest man in the world'.[36] Briggs recalled that, as with Lend Lease, 'most of the marketing people were ex-radio hams'.[37] Like Lend Lease and the other major firms, Westfield transitioned from promotions to marketing.[38] Reg Jebb, who began his retail property market research career in the 1960s, argued that this was a straightforward business decision: promotion-oriented marketing 'would fill the shopping centre for a while. Then everybody would dissipate'.[39] Promotions proved 'absolutely incidental to the business... [They caused] too many traffic jams in the middle of the mall and the shoppers could not get around and the businesses were adversely affected by it'.[40] Promotions also told retail property managers very little about their customers, nor what they needed in terms of a retail offer.

Traditionally, Lloyd argued, there was minimal research undertaken before a shopping centre was built. Developers would simply look for a site where there were '200,000 people who haven't got a shopping centre?'.[41] Michael Lonie suggested that 'a lot of it in days gone by was [done] on gut feeling'.[42] Mark Fookes, Chief Financial Officer for GPT, claimed that 'years ago, some of the guys ... did a commercial assessment on the back of their business card'. Westfield co-founder, John Saunders, allegedly selected sites by driving around cities in a taxi looking for vacant land.[43] His employee, Alan Briggs, declared that suburban consumers in the 1960s were so underserviced with shops that they would visit 'a dog box in the middle of a paddock somewhere'.[44]

These were all exaggerations that perpetuated an industry-friendly story of courageous capitalistic endeavour. This story echoed the praise visited on shopping centre developers by the media and politicians during the 1960s. When Roselands opened in Sydney's southwest in 1965, one newspaper claimed that 'the visitor's first reaction is to wonder ... at the sort of courage that was needed to sink £six million into a spot by-passed by commerce'.[45] Elsewhere, developers were praised for their 'rock courage', vision, and enterprise for risking enormous sums of money on retail developments that transformed underdeveloped suburbs.[46] The idea that such investments were founded on 'gut instinct' rather than solid research feeds into this story of bravado and visionary business enterprise.

The possibility of succeeding without solid research, however, also points to the very real opportunities available in the early days of shopping centre development in Australia. The huge growth of suburban populations and the shift to car-driving shopping created enormous pressure for investments in retail infrastructure. Established strip shopping precincts required car-parking stations. Public authorities were slow to develop these, while many councils saw the private development of shopping centres as a solution to the problem.[47] There was also demand from shoppers for modern retail facilities.[48] Although suitable land with appropriate land-use zoning could be difficult to acquire, the conditions were generally favourable for development. In this environment, developer entrepreneurs relied on observation, logic, and knowledge obtained from retailers who understood their markets.

The larger retail firms, though, did seek to gain an understanding of the markets in which they pursued developments. Myer, for example, engaged economic consultants to help it select sites around Melbourne in the late-1950s as it began to plan its move into shopping centre construction. Analysis was undertaken on population growth, spending patterns, transportation networks, and the relative intensity of Myer customers in given areas.[49] The challenge lay in the accuracy and depth of the data. Gaps between government censuses could mean that data about population sizes, incomes, and spending patterns were several years out of date. Further, if a potential greenfield site had little established housing around it, it was very difficult to estimate its local market's future demographic composition and even harder to measure potential shopping expenditure. And while researchers had some indicators about the relationship of income to retail spending, this was based on national rather than local patterns. So even for the largest firms, the data on which development decisions were based was generic and approximate.[50]

By the 1980s, as the proliferation and growing scale of shopping centres brought them into greater competition with one another, it was becoming clear that improved research capabilities offered competitive advantages.[51] Michael Lloyd recalled that at Lend Lease, his boss, Stuart Hornery, came into his office one day and said, 'we've got to get real on marketing ... it's all got to be real marketing and not promotions'.[52] Hornery, a civil engineering graduate who had become the chief executive of Lend Lease at only 39 years of age,[53] wanted marketing 'to be all about future directions and what people are doing, consumer habits and social demographic composition'.[54] Hornery told Lloyd and Clarke to replace the older generation of promotion-oriented marketers with young marketing graduates. They did so, placing them inside shopping centres to give them direct experience. This, Clarke said, exposed them to 'the community, the retailers ... the security aspect of the building ... [and] all the numbers'.[55] Lend Lease wanted its future executives to understand the operational aspects of shopping centre management before they took up dedicated marketing roles.

Lloyd noted that as these graduates progressed in their careers, they 'brought a whole new view on marketing'.[56] Part of this derived from their education, but technology also expanded the parameters of their profession. When Tony Dimasi began his research career as a consultant to development firms, there were no computers, and all calculations were done on a Hewlett-Packard HP12 Calculator. His company's first word-processor 'was the size of a household fridge'.[57] As computers were introduced, researchers were able to build far more complex and fine-grained models of consumer spending.[58] This capacity to process and interrogate data, in turn, encouraged the acquisition of yet more data. Shopping centre leases in Australia have almost always required tenants to report their sales figures to landlords because rents comprised a base rate plus a proportion of turnover. This sales data offered valuable information, not only about the performance of individual retailers, but also about spending patterns across a range of product categories in any particular market.[59] Expenditure data like this is now collated into a shared resource of industry-wide benchmarks that are fed back to the contributing shopping centre owners.[60]

This is another example of the continuing professionalisation of the industry. We've seen that industry leaders understood the need to reform behaviours that had arisen in the frontier stage of shopping centre construction; practices that flourished when scrutiny was not applied to chains of command became business liabilities as the industry matured. In the case of market research, oral histories show that over time, industry leaders became deeply attached to fine-grained market research data because the margin for error when undertaking developments had shrunk as competition and the scale of investment had grown. These were the same executives who came into the industry in the 1980s when firms such as Lend Lease were replacing 'radio hams' with marketing graduates. Along their career paths to CEO, CFO, or national marketing and development leadership roles, they developed close working relationships with specialist research firms. The careers of today's industry leaders thus evolved alongside the progressive acquisition of deeper data.[61] With this experience, they proved able to articulate and mobilise cooperative practices between firms to produce an industry-wide retail sales database that offered enormous benefits. These included deep insights into the market value of shopping centre space; the performance of tenants with whom leasing negotiations took place; the future spending patterns of trade areas; the relative demand for products, stores, and services in these trade areas; and the optimal scale and retail mix of new and redeveloped shopping centre sites. Retailer databases like this are now supplemented with big data sets garnered from credit cards which firms are 'able to adapt ... into really useful research that can be applied to shopping centre developments and repositioning exercises'.[62]

Understanding the Customer

The many business advantages of deep market research are not the most prominent narrative themes when industry executives discuss the topic. Instead, they talk about 'understanding the customer' and serving the community. This has become the explanatory framework for the success of shopping centres in Australia. By couching the pursuit of business goals within an ethic of customer service, the industry links development with public interest and positions innovation as a response to community needs. Such framing provides a limited picture that redacts other elements of the history and can be seen as part of the industry's image rehabilitation since the damaging accusations about tenant exploitation that sparked leasing legislation in the 1980s.

Whether developments were undertaken on 'gut feel' or guided by a sophisticated analysis of complex data sets, interviewees insisted that shopping centres have remained relevant to shoppers throughout their history because of their flexibility and ability to adapt to changing circumstances. In his interview, Greg Chubb, Retail CEO at Charter Hall, declared that 'if you do not continue to adapt and change in retail, as a retailer or as an owner of retail real estate, you will die ... It is really a relevance issue, and it is a reinvention thing'.[63] Another suggested that 'obviously if something stood still as life changes, it would become irrelevant and obsolete'.[64] In his appraisal of the industry's history, Tony Dimasi argued that:

> the recurring theme is the flexibility and adaptability of Australian shopping centres ... Every step of the way, they might have come across a bit of a rough patch, but they adapt, and they change. This is exactly what has happened and what continues to happen to this day.[65]

For Chubb, this has meant providing the appropriate retail mix for 'the market in which you will be operating, whether it be from a supply and demand point of view or a socio-economic point of view'.[66] This has produced subtle differences in the retail mix of shopping centres depending on the trade areas in which they operate. But because of the size of the Australian market, the constraints placed on stand-alone developments by planning regimes, the historical desire of most large retail chains to locate within shopping centres, and the homogeneity of the broad middle market in Australia, it has also meant that most Australian shopping centres facilitate a broad range of shopping activities. Tony Dimasi argued that:

The one thing that our shopping centres have always been, is very responsive. I suppose they've had to be. Australia is a pretty small place, it's not a mass-market or a huge market. We've only got 20-odd million people so ... the centres have had to be ... almost a jack-of-all-trades.[67]

So, while tenancy mixes were curated to align with local markets, the Australian shopping centre model includes, almost by default, most major retailers other than those selling bulky goods.

This multi-layered shopping centre model was a response to customer shopping patterns. It was also a product of local conditions and driven by the needs of large retailers. Supermarkets were introduced to Australia at the same time as the first shopping centres were being built. Developers offered supermarket operators good sites with car parking in suburban locations. They could also provide local expertise and used connections with local authorities to obtain planning approvals that helped facilitate the national expansion of chains such as Coles that started in Victoria, and initially struggled to break into the large New South Wales market.[68] Department stores also actively participated in development. They built the largest early shopping centres to facilitate suburban branch store expansion, grow their market share, and out-compete rivals. Even those department stores that didn't undertake development themselves found advantages in outsourcing site selection, development approvals, design and construction to other firms and entrepreneurs. These stores joined shopping centres as tenants.[69] Michael Lloyd argued that 'the developers said, "what do you want?" And the department store gave them the specification. The supermarkets gave them the specification'.[70] Because these nascent supermarkets offered a limited range of goods, the developers also petitioned established local retailers like grocers, butchers, fish shops, and delicatessens to open stores. When they incorporated specialty fashion stores into the retail mix, developers targeted middle of the road, utilitarian chains selling children's clothing, workwear, and middle-of-the-road fashion. Michael Lloyd argued that this meant that Australian 'centres provided the retail needs of the community. Whereas the American centres provided the retail wants'.[71] Expanding on this, he claimed that the American mall was:

primarily luxury and leisure orientated. Major department stores, which were fashion orientated; beauticians, hairdressers; specialty shops; jewellers; personal grooming; cafes; restaurants. That was it. No supermarkets or food. No nothing, just luxury items. Now the act of driving a car, a big car, down [to] the mall; down the freeway to the mall was a highly pleasurable experience. And, once you got there, your parking was easy. You were in piped music ... you took more care over your dress when you were going to the mall because it was a luxury place. It was opulent and it was extravagant.[72]

Early shopping centre advertising and architecture in Australia sought to capture some of this allure. Modernist sculptures, fountains, and landscaped central courts became standard features of large-scale developments in the 1960s.[73] Roselands, Sydney's biggest early regional centre opened in 1965 and became famous for its Raindrop Fountain, which used a special liquid running down hundreds of thin nylon threads to create the illusion of a 'seeping rain forest'. Nearby, a giant rose comprised 15 hand-beaten copper petals revolving under a deluge of water jets that run into a pool beneath a suspended fashion catwalk.[74] A lush indoor garden surrounded, connected, and softened these disparate modernist flourishes, which were used to promote the idea that shopping could be a leisure activity and not a chore.[75] Advertisements for Roselands and other centres that featured similar, if less grand, modernist artefacts invited shoppers to 'step into tomorrow', into 'a new way of life'.[76]

Because of their retail mixes, however, Australian shopping centres were also highly utilitarian. Their character was established early, when Australian developers integrated supermarkets in the first shopping centres, and continued as new retail formats building on supermarket logics and aesthetics were introduced to the country. During the 1970s and 1980s, Australia's three largest retailers, Coles, Woolworths and Myer, all introduced DDSs.[77] This highly rationalised retail format applied self-service to department store goods. Stores were single floor, with wide aisles to accommodate shopping trolleys. Chains relied on scale turnover and operational efficiencies to support low margin selling that undercut traditional stores on price. The initial preference of firms was to build stand-alone DDS stores along the American model, but planning approvals were very difficult to obtain for individual stores located on cheap land beyond established retail precincts. As a result, shopping centres again became vehicles for retail chain expansion. DDSs opened in established shopping centres, but also became anchors for a new shopping centre format, the sub-regional centre. These effectively replaced earlier shopping centres that were anchored by variety or small department stores, both of which were rendered obsolete by DDSs and supermarkets. Sub-regional centres were neither opulent nor extravagant. They were highly utilitarian with architecture reflecting their role as functional distribution points for discount retailing. As these shopping centres were redeveloped to grow with their surrounding markets, they, in turn, broadened their retail scope encompassing not only supermarkets and DDSs, but services, and a growing range of specialty shops.[78]

From the mid-1980s onwards, a wave of redevelopments saw many shopping centres across the country expanded to include an even greater range of functions. This was conditioned by two structural shifts: the deregulation of retail trading hours and a shift in consumption expenditure from goods to services. At the beginning of the decade, big retailers in Australia began seriously agitating for longer shopping hours, comparing their own restrictive trading hours to the greater freedoms available to their contemporaries in the United States and Europe. Many viewed their sites as underutilised, lying idle for 16 hours a day, most of the week, and barely used on the weekends.[79] The resultant, progressive extension of shop trading hours allowed landlords to work their sites harder and to respond to a drift in consumer expenditure towards services and leisure experiences.[80]

Reflecting on the need to constantly update retail facilities, John Schroder, CEO of Retail at Stockland, asked rhetorically,

> when you think about it, about how long do you think these bloody [shopping centre] things last? There's a finite timeframe when they become obsolete. You either have to address it and redevelop them, or ... demolish the whole thing.[81]

To maintain relevance, take advantage of the new wider trading hours, and capture a larger share of leisure expenditure developers from the late 1980s onwards undertook significant rebuilds and redevelopments to incorporate multiplex cinemas, games arcades, and food courts. Cinema screens at the time were heavily concentrated in urban centres. Exhibitors, under pressure from the evolution of home video, sought sites in suburban locations with car parking. Shopping centres welcomed them as a means of extending the operating hours of their facilities and a way to attract more customers who could be encouraged to shop before or after watching movies.[82] Food courts kept people in centres for longer, which also increased shopping activity.[83] Design was elevated in these flagship centres, restoring a commitment to amenity that had been lost under the rational utility of DDS-based developments. Graham Terry, who worked in the Myer property portfolio, argued that this 'all-encompassing model was the best [shopping centre] recipe in the world'.[84]

Creating Community Centres and Retail Town Halls

Outside of major redevelopments, social and technological changes produced obsolescence as well as new opportunities for re-mixing retail. According to former Director of Strategy and Property at Coles Myer, Andrew Scott, this was because shopping centres 'have to be dynamic in responding to the local community in changing the content of that shopping centre'. Scott gave the example of a saddlery business, which 50 years ago might have traded well, but clearly had little relevance today. Mobile phone stores, in contrast, he pointed out, sold an entirely new product category and were now essential in any shopping centre. A landlord who did not include a mobile phone store today was 'just not responding to the community'.[85]

In several interviews, executives made intrinsic connections between market research, understanding the customer, meeting community needs, and the role of shopping centres as community hubs. This reflected a shared idea about the nature of the shopping centre that came to permeate the industry. Michael Lloyd claimed that:

> Lend Lease was the first one to find this out. There was a phrase I used for a paper I wrote for the corporation ... I said: the shopping centre ought to become the 'community focal point'... if you've got a place and the community just came there – like they would just go to the town square or the main street or whatever – if that was a place that they just gravitated to ... you made more money than you did if it was just the retail facility.[86]

Other executives argued that shopping centres were successful because they 'were able to satisfy the community's demand'.[87] Redevelopments to expand centres to include more shops, for example, were described as responses to the needs of surrounding communities that had been identified through market research. This produced ever larger centres that dominated retail geographies. While this could be seen as:

> trying to monopolise that community ... in fact, it is simply that they wanted to have every shopper in the area in their centres. It's their philosophy and it's one which made sense. It effectively got more of the community in that area to come into the centre.[88]

The notion that shopping centres catered to the needs of the community led to a rhetorical slippage, with executives describing them as a type of public civic space. This idea probably originated with Victor

Gruen, one of the founding architects of shopping mall design in America, who promoted malls as the modern equivalent of the medieval market square.[89] The idea was reproduced in 1960s Australian promotional material,[90] and later aligned neatly with the idea of shopping centres as community spaces. Michael Lonie, who worked for Westfield for many years, argued that 'the shopping town was where you came to shop. It was a town in itself'.[91] And as the shopping centre's functions broadened, it did begin to resemble an actual town. Michael Lloyd declared that the shopping centre is like 'your original village square. The more successful this centre becomes the more it assumes that right. The property value ... all roads led there'.[92]

Turning shopping centres into town centres became a key goal of the industry. Peter Holland argued that:

> we can incorporate libraries, we can incorporate gymnasiums, we can incorporate leisure and entertainment, we incorporate medical now, we incorporate civic uses ... That's a way that the shopping centre is performing the old town centre, community, civic role as well as a commercial, market role, in exchanging goods and services.[93]

Managing Director of AMP Capital Shopping Centres, Brian Hynes, envisaged 'building communities that live on your doorstep, that have hospitals, student accommodation, hotels and that sort of thing (This means) you're creating towns and really the town centre of tomorrow'.[94] Greg Chubb argued that 'ultimately [the shopping centre] is like the old village square: it is a meeting place [and] you can do everything in one visit'.[95]

The historian Andrew May argues that historical analogies such as these serve a strategic function, providing modern, privatised retail environments with a guise of public space.[96] In America, Lizabeth Cohen suggests that the shopping centre industry promoted malls as community centres, but then defined 'community' in exclusionary socioeconomic terms.[97] Leonie Sandercock argues, for example, that malls offered 'a more perfect downtown' by excluding the weather and traffic, as well as 'poor and coloured folks'.[98] These were commercial decisions to create not a perfect town square, but a perfect selling space. Victor Gruen himself encountered this binary when designing some of his first shopping centres. His plans for non-commercial space and areas set aside for quiet repose ran counter to the inclinations and interests of his developer clients.[99] William H. Whyte argued in the eighties that such delimited environments should not be considered true town centres, because 'they do not welcome – indeed, do not tolerate – controversy, soapboxing, passing of leaflets, impromptu entertaining, happenings, or eccentric behaviour, harmless or no'.[100] Such regulations define shopping centres as private spaces. As Peter Spearritt argues: 'if your access to particular public spaces depends on both your willingness and your ability to pay, then those spaces cease to be public'.[101]

*** *** ***

In the mid-1950s, the retail property industry in Australia did not exist. By the 1980s, it was a dominant force in retailing. Shopping centres were considered the prime sites for most retail functions and there was considerable demand for space within them. Oral histories show that in response to the retail property industry's growing maturity, complexity, and scale, professionalisation was introduced through management training, codes of conduct, improved accountability, and standardised operations. Promotions-based marketing that attracted shoppers through entertainment and gimmicks began to be replaced by professional market research. This targeted shoppers by more effectively tailoring retail solutions to their shopping and spending patterns. Interviewees indicated a prevailing view that the industry survived and thrived by continually adapting shopping centre formats to meet customer demand, incorporating additional functions like food and entertainment, and accommodating disruptive retail business models. This did more than buffer retail property against the creative destruction that was transforming retailing; it allowed retail property managers to benefit from disruptors by renting retail space to them in place of retail formats or brands that lost relevance. In this account, stability was achieved by absorbing constant change.

In addition to providing considerable details about these historical developments, oral histories with retail property executives reveal how the industry pictures itself and how it presents this image to outsiders. The impacts of shopping centre dominance, including declining high streets and spiralling occupancy costs for smaller tenants, are obscured in a shared industry narrative that links market success with a capacity to meet community needs. Oral histories show the historical evolution of this narrative in a way that other sources cannot. When specialty retail tenants complained of mistreatment and began agitating for reform in the 1980s, shopping centre landlords not only professionalised their management practices, but also re-crafted a story about their social role. This began with the precept that 'understanding the customer' was the essential ingredient for retail success. When it became understood that marketing retail sites as community hubs produced sound investment returns, industry rhetoric shifted accordingly, insisting that shopping centre innovation and growth was a response to community needs. As developers further expanded the function of shopping centres to attract more custom, the idea of shopping centres as 'town halls' became a common catch phrase. The value of oral history here lies in its capacity to chart the iterative development of a legitimising narrative that has become an industry-wide mantra, while simultaneously garnering the expertise and knowledge of managers accumulated across their working lives.

Notes

1 Richard Clarke, interview by Matthew Bailey, 24 March 2015.
2 Michael Lloyd, interview by Matthew Bailey, 11 June 2014.
3 Renato Rosaldo, 'Doing Oral History', *Social Analysis: The International Journal of Anthropology*, no. 4 (1980): 89.
4 Barbie Zelizer, 'Reading the Past against the Grain: the Shape of Memory Studies', *Critical Studies in Mass Communication* 12, no. 2 (1995): 214.
5 Per H. Hansen, 'Business History: A Cultural and Narrative Approach', *Business History Review* 86, no. 4 (2012): 700.
6 Portia Dilena, '"Listening Against the Grain": Methodologies in Uncovering Emotions in Oral History Interviews', *Oral History Australia Journal* no. 41 (2019): 43–49.
7 Mike Zundel, Robin Holt and Andrew Popp, 'Using History in the Creation of Organizational Identity', *Management & Organizational History* 11, no. 2 (2016): 212.
8 Pierre Volle, 'Rhetorical History and Strategic Marketing: the Example of Starbucks', *Journal of Historical Research in Marketing* 14, no. 1 (2022): 111–29.
9 Beverley Kingston, *Basket, Bag and Trolley: A History of Shopping in Australia* (Melbourne: Oxford University Press, 1994), 94–108; Lindsay Barrett, 'Roselands, or Everything Under One Roof', *UTS Review* 4, no. 2 (1998) 123–38; Peter Spearritt, 'I Shop Therefore I Am', in *Suburban Dreaming: An Interdisciplinary Approach to Australian Cities*, ed. L. C. Johnson (Geelong: Deakin University Press, 1994), 134–35.
10 J. Ross McKeever, Frank H. Spink, Nathaniel M. Griffin and Urban Land Institute (U.S.), *Shopping Center Development Handbook* (Washington, DC: Urban Land Institute, 1977), 4–7.
11 JLW Research and Consultancy, 'Examining Investment in Community Shopping Centres', Property Research Paper, September 1993, 3.
12 Nigel Flannigan, 'Life for Traditional Shopping Streets: Avoiding the 'Quick-Fix' Solution', *Landscape Australia* 11, no. 3 (1989): 283–94.
13 Westfield Holdings Ltd., *The Westfield Story: The First 40 Years* (Sydney: Westfield Holdings, c2000); Matthew Bailey, 'Power, Politics and

Payments in Pot Plants: Shopping Centre Development in Bankstown 1955–2005', *Melbourne Historical Journal* 33 (2005): 13–24.

14 Matthew Bailey, *Managing the Marketplace: Reinventing Shopping Centres in Post-War Australia* (Routledge: London, 2020), 22–40.

15 Modern Merchandising Methods (MMM), *Australian Shopping Centres* (Australia: MMM, 1971); Matthew Bailey, 'Urban Disruption, Suburbanization and Retail Innovation: Establishing Shopping Centres in Australia', *Urban History* 47, no. 1 (2020): 152–69.

16 *Inside Retailing*, 9 May 1983, 11; 9 April 1984, 1; 16 September 1985, 7; 2 December 1985, 3; 19 May 1986, 1. See also, *The Retail Trader*, January 1989, 1, and Matthew Bailey, '"Feudal Barons Extracting Tribute:" Narratives of Market Power in the Australian Retail Property Sector during the 1980s', *Enterprise and Society* (E-pub ahead of print, 2021).

17 Bailey, *Managing the Marketplace*, 133–36.

18 Robert Spector, *Category Killers: The Retail Revolution and Its Impact on Consumer Culture* (Boston, MA: Harvard Business School Press, 2005); Patrick Hyder Patterson, 'The Supermarket as a Global Historical Development', in *The Routledge Companion to the History of Retailing*, ed. Jon Stobart and Vicki Howard (Abingdon; New York: Routledge, 2019), 154–79.

19 *Inside Retailing* 16 September 1985, 7. See also, *The Retail Trader*, January 1989, 1; A. White, Queensland Legislative Assembly, 26 November 1981, 4080; John Innes, Queensland Legislative Assembly, 26 November 1981, 4088; John Goleby, Queensland Legislative Assembly, 26 November 1981, 4086.

20 *Inside Retailing*, 7 February 1983, 6; 21 March 1983, 3; 23 January 1984, 12; 16 April 1984, 16; 21 May 1984, 12; 18 February 1985, 5.

21 Clarke, interview.

22 *Inside Retailing*, 13 September 1982, 11; 11 April 1983, 3; 2 June 1986, 3; 15 December 1986, 25; Alan Briggs, interview by Matthew Bailey, 26 June 2014.

23 *Inside Retailing*, 3 September 1979, 10; 21 April 1980, 11; 16 August 1982, 3.

24 Neil Crosby, *An Evaluation of the Policy Implications for the UK of the Approach to Small Business Tenant Legislation in Australia* (Reading: University of Reading, 2006), 16; *Inside Retailing*, 6 August 1979, 11; 21 March 1983, 3; 30 January 1984, 2.

25 Bailey, '"Feudal Barons Extracting Tribute"'.

26 Ian Newton, interview by Matthew Bailey, 26 June 2014.

27 *Ibid.*

28 Geoffrey Muntz, Queensland Legislative Assembly, 26 November 1981, 4091; M. T. Williams, Victoria Legislative Assembly, 2 December 1983, 2667; John Klunder, South Australian Legislative Assembly, 26 February 1985, 2859.

29 *Ibid.*

30 *Inside Retailing*, 1 February 1982, 14; 12 April 1982, 6; 16 August 1982, 3.

31 *Inside Retailing*, 12 April 1982, 6; 17 January 1983, 16; 24 June 1985, 14; *BOMA (NSW) News*, May 1985, 20; Briggs, interview.

32 Bailey, '"Feudal Barons Extracting Tribute"'; Adrian J., Bradbrook and Clyde E. Croft, *Commercial Tenancy Law in Australia*, 2nd ed. (North Ryde, NSW: Butterworths, 1997), 519–20, 557–58, 575–76.

33 Clarke, interview.

34 Lloyd, interview.
35 *Ibid.*
36 Newton, interview.
37 Briggs, interview.
38 Newton, interview.
39 *Ibid.*
40 Reg Jebb, interview by Matthew Bailey, 23 February 2015.
41 Lloyd, interview.
42 Michael Lonie, interview by Matthew Bailey, 20 December 2013.
43 Briggs, interview.
44 *Ibid.*
45 Lindsay Barrett, 'Roselands or Everything under One Roof', *UTS Review* 4, no. 2 (1998): 126.
46 *St. George and Sutherland Shire Leader* (Hurstville ed.), 18 March 1964, p. 5; *Sydney Morning Herald*, 20 September 1966, 4, 22; *Sydney Morning Herald*, 21 September 1966, Bankstown Square Feature, 6; *Bankstown Observer*, 21 September 1966, 2–3.
47 Terrence W. Beed, 'The Growth of Suburban Retailing in Sydney: A Preliminary Study of Some Factors Affecting the Form and Function of Suburban Shopping Centres', PhD thesis, University of Sydney, 1964, 95–98.
48 Justine Lloyd & Lesley Johnson, 'Dream Stuff: The Postwar Home and the Australian Housewife, 1940–1960', *Environment and Planning D: Society and Space* 22, no. 2 (2004): 257.
49 *Retail Merchandiser*, May 1960, 8–10; CMA, SLV, Box 1429, Letter from Larry Smith & Company to George McMahon, 22 December 1958; Andrew Hutson, '"I Dream of Jeannie?" the American Origins of the Chadstone Shopping Centre', *Fabrications* 9, no. 1 (May 1999): 23–24.
50 Simon Rumbold, interview by Matthew Bailey, 2 November 2014.
51 Lloyd, interview; *Inside Retailing*, 21 July 1986, 16; Coles Myer Archive, State Library of Victoria, MS13468, *GRACS012, 69*, 'Westfield Shoppingtown Parramatta Store Report', 1979, 1.
52 Lloyd, interview.
53 No author, 'OBITUARY: Stuart Hornery', *Newcastle Herald*, 31 March 2013, https://www.newcastleherald.com.au/story/1399955/obituary-stuart-hornery/
54 Lloyd, interview.
55 Clarke, interview.
56 Lloyd, interview.
57 Tony Dimasi, interview by Matthew Bailey, 3 November 2014.
58 Simon Rumbold, interview by Matthew Bailey, 2 November 2014.
59 Donald W. Burnett, *Shopping Centre Management: The Shopping Centre Lease* (Sydney: Building Owners & Managers Association of Australia, 1981), 9–10; *Inside Retailing*, 6 October 1980, 7.
60 Rumbold, interview; Peter Holland, interview by Matthew Bailey, 18 November 2014.
61 Greg Chubb, interview by Matthew Bailey, 18 March 2015.
62 *Ibid.*
63 *Ibid.*
64 Mark Fookes interview by Matthew Bailey, 6 November 2014.

65 Dimasi, interview.
66 Chubb, interview.
67 Dimasi, interview.
68 Westfield Holdings Ltd., *The Westfield Story: The First 40 Years* (Sydney: Westfield Holdings, c2000), 33.
69 Bailey, 'Urban Disruption', 152–69.
70 Lloyd, interview.
71 *Ibid.*
72 *Ibid.*
73 Janina Gosseye and Peter Vernon, 'Shopping Towns Australia, 1957–67: From Reformist Figure of Collectivity to Profit-Driven Box of Gold', paper presented at the Society of Architectural Historians, Australia and New Zealand, Melbourne, 2016.
74 *Retail Merchandiser*, November 1965, 29–30.
75 CMA, SLV, Box 1946, *Chadstone News*, no. 3, c1960; *Retail Merchandiser*, May 1960, 12; Canterbury City Council Library, Local Studies Collection, Roselands File, 'Everything for Everybody at Grace Bros Roselands'.
76 *The Torch*, 20 October 1965, n.p.; A.G Sloan, 'Marion – a 'One-Stop' Shopping Centre', *Journal of Industry* 36, no. 4 (1968): 25.
77 Matthew Bailey, 'Absorptive Capacity, International Business Knowledge Transfer, and Local Adaptation: Establishing Discount Department Stores in Australia', *Australian Economic History Review* 57, no. 2 (2017): 194–216.
78 Dimasi, interview.
79 *Business Review Weekly*, 8–14 October 1983, 42; *Australian Business*, 16 July 1981, 74; CMA, SLV, Memo from B. P. Sloan, Results of discussion with Mr R. Aitchison and ACAM, 28 August 1981; CMA, SLV, Box 1166, Major convenience stores operating extended trading hours, c. 1980–1982; Kingston, *Basket Bag and Trolley*, 114; Robert G.V. Baker, '"What Hours Should We Trade, Mr Superstore?:" A Review of the 1994 Australian Experience', *Urban Policy and Research* 13, no. 2 (1995): 90–100.
80 *ABS Household Expenditure Survey 2009–2010: Summary of Results*, 6530.0 (Canberra, 2011), 30; Amy Beech, Rosetta Dollman, Richard Finlay and Gianni La Cava, 'The Distribution of Household Spending in Australia', *Reserve Bank of Australia Bulletin*, March Quarter 2014, https://www.rba.gov.au/publications/bulletin/2014/mar/2.html
81 John Schroder, interview by Matthew Bailey, 4 March 2015.
82 Matthew Bailey, 'Shopping for Entertainment: Malls and Multiplexes in Sydney, Australia', *Urban History* 42, no. 2, (2015): 309–29.
83 Kim Humphery, *Shelf Life: Supermarkets and the Changing Cultures of Consumption* (Cambridge, Melbourne: Cambridge University Press, 1998), 153; Peter H. Bloch, Nancy M. Ridgway and Scott A. Dawson, 'The Shopping Mall as Consumer Habitat', *Journal of Retailing* 70, no. 1 (1994): 30.
84 Graham Terry, interview by Matthew Bailey, 18 February 2015.
85 Andrew Scott, interview by Matthew Bailey, 31 March 2015.
86 Lloyd, interview.
87 Scott, interview.

88 *Ibid.*
89 Victor Gruen and Larry Smith, *Shopping Towns USA: The Planning of Shopping Centers* (New York: Reinhold, 1960), 17–24.
90 Advertisement in *The Advocate*, 16 October 1968, 10.
91 Lonie, interview.
92 Lloyd, interview.
93 Holland, interview.
94 Brian Hynes, interview by Matthew Bailey, 2 March 2015.
95 Chubb, interview.
96 Andrew Brown-May, *Melbourne Street Life: The Itinerary of Our Days* (Kew: Australian Scholarly Publishing, 1998), 120.
97 Lizabeth Cohen, 'From Town Center to Shopping Center: The Reconfiguration of Community Marketplaces in Postwar America', *The American Historical Review* 101, no. 4 (1996): 1059. See also, Rob White and Adam Sutton, 'Social Planning for Mall Redevelopment: An Australian Case-Study', *Local Environment* 6, no. 1 (2001): 69; Andrew Allan, 'Marion: A Study of a Super-Regional Centre and its Impact on Adelaide', *Urban Policy and Research* 16, no. 2 (1998): 124.
98 Leonie Sandercock, 'From Main Street to Fortress: The Future of Malls as Public Spaces – OR – "Shut Up and Shop"', *Just Policy*, no. 9 (1997), 28. See also Anne Friedberg, 'Les Flâneurs du Mall (1): Cinema and the Postmodern Condition', *PMLA* 106, no. 3 (1991): 419–31; Lizabeth Cohen, *A Consumers' Republic: The Politics of Mass Consumption in Postwar America* (New York: Vintage Books, 2003), 265; Brown-May, *Melbourne Street Life*, 215.
99 Victor Gruen, 'The Sad Story of Shopping Centres', *Town and Country Planning*, no. 46 (1978): 350–52; M. Jeffrey Hardwick, *Mall Maker: Victor Gruen, Architect of an American Dream* (Philadelphia: University of Pennsylvania Press, 2004), 219.
100 William H. Whyte, *City* (New York: Doubleday, 1988), 208. See also Michael Webb, *The City Square: A Historical Evolution* (London: Thames & Hudson, 1990), 206.
101 Peter Spearritt, 'Suburban Cathedrals: The Rise of the Drive-In Shopping Centre', in *The Cream Brick Frontier: Histories of Australian Suburbia*, ed. Graeme Davison, Tony Dingle and Seamus O'Hanlon (Clayton: Monash Publications in History, 1995), 96.

4   Digital Disruption
The Advertising Industry's
Uneasy Revolution

In the mid-1990s, it was becoming clear that the internet was something that needed to be taken seriously. Many recognised its transformative potential, but few could envisage the form of this creative destruction let alone its extent. Writing in his regular column for an Australian advertising trade publication, Haydon Bray offered a colourful account of the situation in business circles:

> Business and the Internet are like teenagers and sex. Everyone's obsessed with it. Everyone thinks everyone else does it. Everyone wants everyone else to think they do it, too. But hardly anyone really does it, and most of them do it badly.[1]

Similar views were expressed by Rob Oliver, whose agency held the Microsoft account:

> There's a lot of talk about the information superhighway, there's a lot of talk about hot technology ... but cut through the bullshit and you soon find there's more hype than realism ... it's time to look at what can be done.[2]

Looking back on this period in an interview almost 25 years later, Dominic Pearman, the head of an independent media agency, also noted the excitement surrounding the new medium. However, Pearman mused that this hype was also being fuelled by other interests:

> And I think only now that businesses really understand the role of digital, whereas before it was more of a ... driven by the media. And if you look at the trade press, it would be interesting to look at trade press and look at how much exposure is or was given to digital media versus the traditional, TV, radio, print. [...] So I think it

DOI: 10.4324/9781003171232-5

was probably driven by the likes of *AdNews, Mumbrella, B&T*, in the media industry to basically give digital a greater importance than probably what it deserved, I think.[3]

While Bray and Oliver certainly shared these sentiments, the trade press' publication of their views nevertheless helped reinforce the perception that Pearman held. This unique situation not only provides a deeper insight into the internet's arrival in the advertising and marketing sector but also invites us to consider the ways that oral history can challenge documentary evidence.

In their chapter on business history agendas, historiography, and debates for the *Routledge Companion to Business History*, Steven Toms and John Wilson position archival and case study research as the 'conventional' approach for business historians. Archival materials, they argue, need to be verified by other sources, including the press and oral history. However, Toms and Wilson go on to express reservations about the use of oral testimony. Sounding an 'academic health warning', they caution that 'the propensity of some individuals to relate a narrative that does not necessarily tally with the written record' can create 'major problems for the historian when attempting to produce an objective conclusion'.[4] While this critique is certainly valid, the authors are conspicuously silent on the shortcomings of the other point of verification – the press. The press and, in particular, trade publications are integral resources for business historians, offering broader context on the one hand and additional detail and insight on the other. As such, they need to be subjected to the same level of critical evaluation as any other resource. Although the press has been subjected to countless critiques, the trade press has largely been ignored. Media scholars Kenton Wilkinson and Patrick Merle thus assert that 'researchers should devote greater attention to the benefits and potential pitfalls of using business press and industry trade journal reports to inform academic research'.[5] Of the pitfalls identified by Wilkinson and Merle, two stand out. With a narrow focus and a restricted market (in terms of readership, information sources, and potential advertisers), the trade press can struggle with impartiality. Building on this issue, Wilkinson and Merle call for further work to be done on agenda setting, expressing concerns that the trade press was not simply reporting stories but also actively creating them. It seems that an 'academic health warning' might be equally applicable here. The fact that Wilkinson and Merle's concerns echo Pearman's observations is significant, as it illustrates that oral history is as reliable as other historical sources – a point that this chapter explores.

This chapter seeks to gain a deeper insight into the process of creative destruction by examining the arrival of digital media within the advertising industry in Australia. It provides a comparison between reports in the local trade press and the recollections and views outlined in oral history interviews with advertising professionals who worked in the industry in the 1990s and 2000s. The interviews were undertaken as part of a broader survey documenting the transformation of Australia's advertising during this period.[6] With documentary materials difficult to locate, let alone access, this project drew heavily on the trade press and oral history testimony. Specifically, the chapter asks whether the images conveyed in the trade press were in line with individual recollections about the ways that digital media arrived in the agencies along with its actual impact on the everyday operations of the advertising industry. In addition to revealing the degree of hyperbole surrounding the arrival of digital media, the interviews provide an insight into the organisational and cultural factors that prevented any wholehearted embrace of digital media along with any major disruption wrought by it.

'Wow, how sophisticated is this!?'

When John Sintras first entered the advertising industry in 1982, the state of technology was little better than it had been two decades earlier. Sintras, who commenced his advertising career in the media department of Sydney's Leo Burnett office, recalled that:

> [W]hen I started, we had telex machines, photocopiers, there were no computers. There were typewriters, not even a word processor. Like it was another world. Everything was manual. Telephones, someone called and left a message and you were called on a landline. You could not be contacted at lunch. ... It was mail boys delivering memos. Like it was another time in every way you can possibly imagine.[7]

Two decades later, technology had left an indelible impact on the agency and its operations with computers and email both becoming relatively commonplace at the turn of the century. Recollections of the uptake of such technologies, however, reveal that their arrival was a slow, uneven process.

The simple, low-tech office outlined by Sintras may have been an accurate portrait of Leo Burnett, but it was not necessarily the situation across all Australian agencies. Large agencies had in fact been investing in computers since the 1960s, possessing both the capital to invest in such expensive machinery and the physical space to accommodate such giant new machines. These computers primarily served the agency's administrative departments, notably accounting and media, and would later be used for collating research data.[8] Computers would only begin to enter other parts of the agency from the mid-1980s onwards, with Apple leading the way.

Launched with great fanfare in 1984, the Apple Macintosh was perfectly suited to agency work as it supported the work being done by the creative department as well as the administrative work undertaken by other departments. The first converts were not to be found in the large agencies, but rather the smaller, creatively focused agencies, which operated on a much more modest scale. While the new personal computers were still a significant investment, they were notabaly cheaper than previous models and took up less space. Their functionality was also suited to the operational model of the smaller agencies, where staff often worked across the creative-administrative divide. And with fewer people in the agency, everyone had greater access to any new machine than their counterparts in large agencies. John Bevins, who had recently opened his own creative agency, remembered attending the 1985 Caxton Awards' weekend celebration of creativity in print, where one guest speaker urged attendees to buy a new Apple. 'I dutifully went out the next day and bought myself an Apple IIc and started working on that', he recalled.[9] Graham Nunn, another principal of a small creative agency, was also in attendance and was similarly inspired to purchase an Apple. However, Nunn recounted that many in the audience were unconvinced by the promises: 'a lot of people were really sceptical and saying "oh, bullshit, we don't need any computers". But it didn't take long really ... for them to come in and revolutionise [things]'.[10] Reflecting on the computer's impact, Nunn identified an immediate return on investment: 'I've never had a PA or secretary of my own. Computers were the reason you didn't need one'. However, at a creative level, he was more circumspect, noting that he would continue to use a pen and paper before transferring any ideas to the computer.

Despite the growing familiarity with computers and the benefits they offered, the advertising industry as a whole maintained a wary view of the new technology and appeared to be in no rush to embrace it. '[E]ven in the early 90s, the idea of having a computer on the desk was completely foreign', explained Account Director Tony Hale. Such caution does not seem to have been the sole preserve of Australian agencies. Phil Hayden arrived in Australia from Britain in 1989.

Hayden recalled being pleasantly surprised that his new agency had several computers, as his previous agency in the UK had none.[11] By the early 1990s, reports in the trade press indicated that the industry's attitude was beginning to shift with a 1993 article asserting that 'very few [agencies] do not currently have some type of [computer] system installed'.[12] Hale's reaction to seeing his agency embrace computers at this time nevertheless reminds us that the uptake was still slow:

> The Campaign Palace was the first place that I'd ever been to that had a computer on every desk. And I thought at the time—and they were those big clunky Macs—I thought at the time—wow, how sophisticated is this!?[13]

Having a computer or even multiple computers in the office did not necessarily mean that the agency had entered the computer age. As Hale recalled, staff had few of the necessary skills to make the most of the new machines: 'Half of us couldn't type at all. And the idea of having them on the desk was a bit of a folly because nobody knew how to use them'.[14] As a junior dispatch boy at George Patterson in 1994, Paul McMillan saw how the senior members of staff acted as if nothing had changed. McMillan remembered senior members of staff 'who still had secretaries and ... would stand behind them and talk to them and say, can you write this. And they were just clacking away on their typewriters'.[15] John Sintras recounted a similar situation at his agency, but reveals that administrative staff were also actively supporting their Luddite supervisors:

> And there were some people who had secretaries typing their emails for them because they refused, seriously, they refused or didn't know how to use a keyboard, or they were still doing everything handwritten, and passing it to other people to email. I remember secretaries that refused to use a word processor that insisted that they all type and that's all they will do and they refused to change.[16]

Concerns about the computer's impact on jobs were not misplaced. Secretarial staff were the most vulnerable to the new technology. Matt Donovan, who had joined Foote, Cone & Belding (FCB) in 1996 as a 22-year-old Account Director, had a secretary during his first year at the agency. However, he remembered that this experience was short-lived: 'within about a year, the secretaries all disappeared. Only the CEO and the Managing Director had one and the rest of them were all cut out of the business and we all had computers on our desk'.[17] Other positions would similarly disappear. In 1990, Clemenger BBDO's Sydney office, which boasted the Apple account in Australia, updated its production and art department. Within the space of four days, the agency's old art studios were replaced with six Mac workstations. Roger Rigby, who oversaw the upgrade, recalled that younger staff were excited, as 'they were starting to think in computers'. However, some of the older staff failed to embrace the shift, prompting Rigby to issue an ultimatum: '"either you learn it or you go." And I had to fire two people'.[18] Looking back on the demise of the production departments across the industry, Production Staffer Greg McIntyre glumly observed: 'Technology has taken away so many jobs from so many people, and so much craft'.[19] A similar lament was shared by Keith Aldrich, who worked in the creative department. An art director who worked for multiple large agencies, Aldrich found himself dragged into the computer age. He thus explained that up until the 1990s, his briefcase contained 100 magic markers, pentels, pens, and a type-rule for measuring the space between letters:

> And everybody used to say "oh, you're not going to use those anymore – computers are coming", and I'm thinking "I don't want to use a computer, why would I want to use a computer, I just want to draw things out" ... and it went on for years.[20]

However, Aldrich's attitude counted for little. Unable to stem the tide, he eventually found himself learning to use QuarkXPress in order to do his job and to keep up with colleagues:

> So, we were all desperately getting ourselves Mac computers and trying to learn this technology, but not really wanting to because it was far quicker to just scribble it out and present it. But, inevitably, it got more, and more, and more popular.[21]

The impact of such active and passive acts of opposition was effectively undermined by the benefits that computers delivered to agency operations. Over the course of the 1990s, agencies faced greater scrutiny from clients, who were reducing advertising budgets while demanding greater accountability for every dollar that agencies were spending on their behalf. Roger Rigby detailed the computer's enormous impact on his agency's finances vividly. By computerising its production department, Clemenger BBDO Sydney saw its turnover grow from $384,000 annually to $1.2 million within the first 12 months.

In helping to reduce client costs, computers were also increasing the agency's own profitability, as success was now measured by way of the billings to staff ratio. The financial case was further bolstered by the realisation that more could be done for less. John Bevins thus claimed that the computer made his agency: 'intuitively more productive'.[22] The trade press also recognised the value of such insights and duly reported on them.[23] As it became clear that computers were helping to increase profitability and productivity, management began to see the computer as an integral part of agency operations. However, this gradual acceptance of computer technology did not necessarily mean that the advertising industry now embraced it.

'Wondering whether or not it ever got there ...'

When interviewees were asked to outline the way that the internet arrived in their agency, few offered an immediate response. While the process of sifting through memories from decades ago certainly contributed to this pause, it also reflected the challenges around defining the internet and, indeed, its origins. But rather than commenting on the challenge of making sense of websites or dealing with slow connection speeds, their recollections gravitated to a new electronic tool – email. The centrality of email in these recollections was intriguing, as its arrival largely went undocumented in the trade press. A 1997 report on the use of personal computers in *Marketing Week* was one of the few to mention it directly. Expressing some surprise at the growth of email and the fact that a third of users 'now use it from home for both business and personal communication', the article illustrates the communication tool's swift yet inconspicuous spread across the advertising business.[24]

Tom Moult, the Creative Director at Euro RSCG in Sydney, first encountered email in the early 1990s when he was visiting his client Compaq in Houston. He vividly recalled the experience as well as the impression that it left:

> we had a little tech presentation, and at the same meeting, we learnt about email addresses and websites. I remember them saying to me, "So, you'll be tom.moult@something dot, dot, dot," and I'm going, "Yeah, how does this work?" They said, "So, I'll send you a message on the computer," [and] I'm going, "But you don't know where I live." And then they said, "And then there'll be websites, there'll be Tom at dot dot dot com and then they can see." We went away going, "This will never happen".[25]

Moult would not be the only one who struggled to comprehend the difference between digital and analogue modes of communication, nor was he alone dismissing email's potential. Such views appear to have been commonplace in the advertising business. While email was certainly being used by various businesses and organisations in the early 1990s, Australian agencies were by no means early adopters. Most only established email accounts for staff in the second half of the 1990s.

Recollections of the impact of email initially focused on those arcane aspects of agency life that disappeared following the technology's uptake. Ed Brice recalls that when he joined George Patterson Bates in the mid-1990s, internal communications had hardly changed in decades: internal office memos were still the primary mode of communication across the agency. As a young recruit, he was perplexed by the process of placing memos in a tray for someone to carry to another tray just metres away: 'I just thought it was so strange ... Why don't I just go and give it to them, you know. It's like "no, no, you just put it in the out tray. The person will come and pick it up and go and put it in their tray." I'm going, "it's not that far to go!"'.[26] For Kimberlee Wells, a young account manager at Samuelson Talbot & Partners in the late 1990s, it was the replacement of this slow and cumbersome process that stood out in her memories:

> I remember the Teledex notes no longer came on your desk where reception had taken a phone call while you were out, and now all of a sudden it was an email sitting in your inbox. Yes, slips of paper with the clock on it.[27]

Paul McMillan commented on the changing speed of communication. Like Brice, McMillan commenced his advertising career as a dispatch boy at George Patterson in 1995. At that time, his job 'was to hand around inter-office memos through the mail cart in my first year', but by the time he progressed to the next level, the despatch role was already redundant: 'late "95/"96 was when email was on fire and everybody had a computer on their desk and everybody was emailing each other and sitting in their offices'.[28]

As with computers, the advantages derived from introducing email into the agency became clearer once the agency made the leap. Not surprisingly, management and staff alike recognised the efficiencies that email produced. Tony Hale thus outlined the laborious processes that email eliminated: 'rather than handwriting a note and have somebody type it up and put copies all around the office—you could actually, via email, for the first time send stuff to the office, or even external to clients'.[29] The speed of email was recognised as an important advantage in itself. Creative Director Sean Cummins felt that the instantaneous connection wrought by email aided the creative process and built stronger connections between creative teams: 'You could be more organic. You could be faster. And I think just the speed and the ability to communicate faster was a really fantastic thing, and it's always been the case. It's amazing what can be done'.[30] Again, there were those who rebelled at technology's latest incursion into their space. John Sintras remembered that the decision to use email for all internal communication at Leo Burnett 'was not a popular decision in its day' and that some staff who would not or could not comply again looked for ways of avoiding the new technology.[31]

Although interviewees uniformly noted the ways that email enhanced efficiencies across the agencies, their accounts nevertheless revealed that the technology's impact could vary between departments. Staff working in the account service department quickly recognised the benefits of instant communication with their clients. Victor Maree recounted the arrival of email, which enabled him to be in direct contact with one of his agency's new major accounts:

> So I would get back from meeting or something and I'd get a message from Gary "Can you look at blah, blah, blah?" and it was quite amazing. It was a very expensive setup for us, but I have to say that I thought "Look, this is really good."[32]

Maree's anecdote also illustrates the importance of external stakeholders in this process – agencies could not afford to be lagging behind their clients. An unforeseen impact of email on the account management department was its capacity to establish an instant record of discussions and agreements. Prior to the arrival of email, conference reports were produced by account service staff following face-to-face meetings with clients. Sean Cummins recalled that these reports functioned as quasi

> minutes of the meeting but it was also there to just safeguard both sides. And also, to be something that the rest of the agency who may not have been in that meeting could see what was going on and understand it.[33]

Email correspondence both eliminated the need for such documentation and reduced the need for face-to-face meetings and telephone calls as many issues could be efficiently resolved online.

Some agencies only embraced technology once it became clear that existing operations were undermining client relations – an issue that deeply concerned the account service department and, indeed, management. In 1997, Michael McEwen was an account executive at Young & Rubicam's Melbourne office. One of his clients was a retail business based in Sydney, which meant that communication was largely conducted through fax and the newly installed Integrated Services Digital Network (ISDN). The system had several problems. The first was an analogue issue. Although his client had 'beautiful cursive handwriting', McEwen's first task was to decipher what was actually written in the faxes. The next step was to manually produce the advertisement, before faxing or couriering the final product back to Sydney. On one particular occasion, ISDN crashes meant that the electronic artwork could not be sent to Sydney in time for a newspaper deadline. After the wrong images were dispatched by courier, McEwen himself would have to travel to Sydney to hand deliver the correct images. However, the coup de grace was a pricing error that appeared in the printed advertisement. McEwen explained that the series of costly errors compelled the agency to take action:

> And at that stage there was an enquiry into what happened and why did this happen and why did that thing now work? And at that stage, the business said okay, we need to actually work out how we can make this internet thing work. One of the guys at [advertising production house] Show Ads said "Oh we've been testing this high-speed thing where we can actually send an artwork electronically. And we've been trailing it with *Sydney Morning Herald.*" And that was it, that was the catalyst for Show Ads to cease production of bromides and film and actually upgrade the system so they could send material electronically to the newspaper.[34]

Here again, external partners were playing a key role in pushing agencies into the investing in information technology.

Staff working in agency media departments (and in the growing number of media agencies) outlined similar benefits to those identified by account service staff. Imogen Hewitt was a junior media planner/buyer in the media department at FCB in Sydney, and only received her first email address in the late 1990s. She recalls that television spots were still bought by fax, with buyers identifying their preferred spaces and television stations responding with large reports of what was ordered and what was available. As some programmes had 'hundreds of 30-second bits of airtime', staff like Hewitt were given the onerous task of having 'to sit there and, literally with a pen and a ruler, see how close what you'd asked for was replicated in what you got'.[35] Reviews of what actually aired involved a similar process. Hewitt recalled that email not only 'made the transportation of large pieces of paper that you needed to cross reference a little bit easier', but also provided immediate access to media sales staff to query any discrepancies or inconsistencies. While Hewitt admitted that she was 'quite open and willing to embrace anything that seemed like it was going to make things easier', she nevertheless remembered the anxieties surrounding the new technology:

> I remember thinking the first few times I sort of sent emails rather than call someone, or faxed a document, just wondering whether or not it ever got there. Because how do you know? So, I remember that sort of thing. And I remember sometimes calling to make sure that people had got the email that I'd just sent, because you're not quite sure that this thing has actually made it through the ether into the lap of your clients as and when they needed it.[36]

It did not take long for agency staff to become accustomed to using the technology and enjoying the advantages that email offered. However, interviewees reflecting on the past also recognised that the disruptions caused by email were not entirely advantageous. Peter Murphy commenced his advertising career in the pre-email 1980s. Looking back on the impact that email had on agency life, the creative director identified two issues that would have a long-term bearing on agency operations. While email enhanced communication flows between agencies and their clients, it simultaneously reduced personal contact between them. Murphy felt that advertising, as a self-professed 'people business', suffered as a result:

> I think that's a loss for the industry because ... when you're talking to someone, the amount of information you get from their body language and all that stuff is enormous. Unless you are an incredibly gifted writer, you will never be able to precisely put that exactly in an email.[37]

Murphy also challenged the view that email was an inherently more accurate form of communication: 'people get the wrong meanings, the right meanings but the wrong outtake'. Less personal contact similarly created further scope for miscommunication. As Sean Cummins mused, 'that was possibly good and possibly bad, depending on what the outcome was'.[38] Another major issue identified by Murphy was the fact that agencies and clients seldom travelled to one another's premises. Murphy remembered previous experiences where client visits had resulted in additional work:

> you'd know what was going on in their business, and they'd give you projects that you didn't even know existed, because they'd see you there. Because, you know, advertising is like one sixtieth of their job, so they weren't thinking about you.[39]

Email was not the sole preserve of business sector. Hotmail, the first free, online-based email service, grew exponentially during the late 1990s. Launched in 1996, it boasted 30 million users across the globe in 1998, a million of whom were located in Australia.[40] As Tony Hale discovered, email eroded the distance that had hitherto separated advertising agencies from the audiences that they hoped to persuade. Hale worked on a campaign to promote Queensland's Hamilton Island as a tourism destination. Part of the campaign was a single outdoor billboard near Sydney airport, which depicted a couple lazing in a rowboat with the headline 'Chronic Fatigue Syndrome'. Hale thought little of it until his email inbox began to fill up with complaints from the public expressing anger at the campaign's treatment of the health condition:

> And I'm getting inundated with these emails. I never know how they got it—but they got my email address. And I'm getting something like 30 emails a day—from all around the world—abusing me and threatening me and calling me a disgrace and saying that they're going to attack my family, and calling me the worst part of Madison Avenue set. Stuff like this ... it was coming from everywhere.[41]

Looking further into the matter, Hale discovered that a website had in fact been created featuring his image, his home address, his phone numbers, and his email. By illustrating the ways in which the speed, efficiency, and ubiquity of email (and the internet) could be harnessed by the public to communicate back to the advertising industry, Hale's experience demonstrates how the traditional broadcast model of communication was being disrupted – a point that was not lost on Hale:

> it became clear to me, at that stage, the power of the internet. And the ability to connect the world from very remote parts. ... it also

gives a voice to the disaffected ... and allows them a platform to disseminate messages that they wouldn't have had in the past.[42]

'Nobody went "Yippee"'

Up until the mid-1990s, discussions of the internet in the trade press had largely been introductory, describing how the new medium worked and offering some predictions as to how it might affect communication processes. Writing in *Ad News* in 1995, Rob Oliver urged the industry to rethink its focus:

> [t]here's a lot of talk about the information superhighway, there's a lot of talk about hot technology ... but cut through the bullshit and you soon find there's more hype than realism ... it's time to look at what can be done.[43]

As Oliver handled the Microsoft account, his call was not without self-interest. However, a discernible shift was occurring in the trade press with articles beginning to pay more attention to the ways that the advertising industry might use the new medium.[44] This shift was also reflected in the publication of books such as *How to Make a Fortune on the Information Superhighway* and *How to Advertise on the Internet*.[45] Although the trade press increasingly underscored the online opportunities for agencies and their clients, the reality was that the advertising industry had not jettisoned its scepticism. John Sintras, who had become the Media Director and General Manager of Leo Burnett Sydney in the 1990s, recalled the advertising industry's overall response to the internet: 'So somewhere the internet was invented and nobody went, "Yippee." Nobody went, "This is amazing." Nobody was super keen to adopt it'.[46] While the reaction was no different to the industry's initial response to computers and email, interviews reveal that such attitudes would also undermine any attempt to engage with the medium in a serious way.

At the turn of the century, large multinational agencies realised that they could no longer ignore the internet. As the Dotcom Boom took off, the fear of missing out led many agencies to pay closer attention to the medium and how it might be integrated into their operations. FCB was one of them. At FCB's 1999 worldwide conference, the head of one of the agency's newly acquired direct marketing agencies addressed delegates about modern marketing's so-called 'three Ds' – data, digital, and direct marketing. Colin Wilson-Brown, the Chief Executive Officer of FCB's Australian offices, attended the conference. He was impressed by the speaker: 'he was a centrepiece of their annual conference. ... And I mean, I sat there thinking "This is fantastic"'.[47] Upon his return to Australia, Wilson-Brown set about implementing what he had heard: 'we created a new department which was essentially the three Ds of data, digital and direct marketing'. Although he noted that there already existed some demand from clients for such services, he nevertheless felt that the agency's initiative could stimulate further business. In addition, 'we thought it would also be ... a differentiator for the agency, you know, in new business growth and that sort of thing'.[48] In terms of his understanding the new medium itself, Wilson-Brown was blunt: 'I mean, I didn't understand anything about it at all'. Few executives could truthfully claim that they did. However, it was Wilson-Brown's 'thirst for knowledge and ... respect for the way the industry was going' that led him to break away from the pack and to take a leap into the unknown.[49]

FCB's entry into the digital space commenced modestly. There was no big announcement in the trade press. Wilson-Brown took inspiration from the way that British agencies had responded to the arrival of television in the 1950s. Matt Donovan recalled Wilson-Brown telling him how the British agencies had 'started by putting one guy, back in those days, in charge of it and learning all about it, and then over time that one person became the creative department'.[50] It would be Donovan himself who was anointed by Wilson-Brown as 'to become the agency's internet guy'. His experience amounted to little more than having interest in the internet and experience of working on IT accounts – of course, few in the industry could boast much more. Although his role was still an informal one, Donovan was sent to FCB's San Francisco offices: 'They had a number of dotcom clients and were leading the way on this new era of online media and so I went over there to learn what they were doing for a few months'. Upon his return, he and Louise Brockbank (who had been recruited from overseas to head the agency's direct marketing operations) established FCBi, the agency's new digital arm. However, Donovan still struggled to be taken seriously by his colleagues, who either did not understand or simply did not care about the new medium. This situation would change when Mike Zeederberg arrived in 2000.

Mike Zeederberg's career in IT commenced in 1996 when he built a website for a London-based law firm. Despite having 'no background in digital, or marketing, or anything else', his website experience saw him recruited to a digital start-up aligned to Batey Ads in Singapore in 1997.[51] In Singapore, Zeederberg was creating CD ROMs and award-winning websites for major brands like Visa and Mercedes.

However, Zeederberg found himself being drawn to the strategic side of the business:

> And so, it sort of evolved into more of an account planning role very quickly, picking up a lot of the "where does digital fit into the overall marketing space?" And importantly, "where does that fit in inside an agency?"– as opposed to just being a sort of, techy delivery-type person.[52]

He then returned to London, where he worked for a direct marketing agency. 'Everybody needed stuff, everybody wanted stuff, and we were producing websites, and email marketing campaigns, and all sorts of stuff around that space', he recalls. The need for this type of work saw the agency grow from three people to 35 in the space of 18 months. Donovan, who had been travelling to London, urged Wilson-Brown to speak to Zeederberg. Zeederberg recalled the meeting, and recounts how Wilson-Brown sold him the agency's vision:

> given that you started up sort of the digital side of ad agencies a couple of times now already, it'd be great for you to come and start up this thing called FCBi. They're setting it up all over the world, so every office needs an FCBi element to it in the agency space.[53]

Zeederberg could see that this opportunity had real global potential.

Shortly after Zeederberg joined FCBi in 2000, Imogen Hewitt joined the team. Her background was in FCB's media department, where she worked as a planner/buyer. Like Donovan, Hewitt did not have any technical background or information technology skills. She recalls that her decision to move across to the fledgling operations was motivated by the feeling that 'there was something on the horizon with the introduction of the internet' and that this new 'interactive' media seemed 'to be changing things pretty quickly'.[54] Her interest in digital media was also piqued by an abiding interest in media consumption patterns and developing a nuanced understanding of the latest developments:

> And if this is the channel or the technology they're moving into, then it would be interesting to see how we go about utilising that for the purposes of getting advertising messages in front of them in an efficient and new kind of way.[55]

Despite the size of FCB's investment in FCBi and the growing popularity of the internet, agency staff remained overwhelmingly indifferent

to the initiative. 'We were very definitely peripheral', observed Zeederberg, 'Nowhere near being the main game'.[56] Such issues were not lost
on Wilson-Brown, who pointed to the problematic attitudes residing
in two key departments:

> The creative people in the main didn't understand it at all. They
> didn't understand the people. They wondered, initially what those
> people doing there because they speak in tongues ... So that was
> complicated. The media department didn't understand it either. I
> mean, they were much more interested, because they could see that
> there were new channels that they needed to understand, but ...
> they'd never seen direct marketing as a channel, for example. It's
> interesting that media people never saw direct marketing as a
> channel ... it wasn't something they needed to be involved in at
> all ...[57]

The creative department's attitude was informed by several factors.
Individual personalities, for example, played a major role. Zeederberg
felt that FCB's creative director was particularly negative: 'he really
didn't want to know what we were doing, [and] wasn't that interested in
anything we were going about'.[58] The creative director's attitude was
also the product of the exalted status of the creative department in the
agency's structural hierarchy. Recalling how 'you would come in and
put forward a creative brief, and go away, and three days later they [the
creative department] would deign to invite you back into their office
to show you the creative concept', Zeederberg recalled that FCBi staff
were actively excluded from the creative process and had little hope of
making any headway unless the creative department changed its view.

FCBi's lowly standing was not necessarily aided by the limitations
of digital advertising. Hewitt thus noted: 'I don't recall having conversations with our creative teams about them being massively enthu-
siastic about what they were going to put in a really small space on a
computer somewhere'. Not only were banners small, 'there wasn't a
great deal of insight as yet into what would make that banner work.
You know, "did someone click it?" [laughs] was about as far as you
got'.[59] However, Hewitt also proffered a further reason for the media
department's reticence. Her sense was that the media department did
not consider it 'a new mass medium' in its own right, and her media
colleagues viewed it as 'an extension of CRM [customer relationship
marketing] or an extension of direct mailers because it was small and
it felt like you could pinpoint particular, I guess, contexts that people were in'.[60] As direct marketers were still derided by many in the

industry as mere envelope fillers, such comparisons reconfirm the medium's lowly status in the agency ranks.[61]

Despite the barriers and hindrances posed by their colleagues in other departments, the FCBi team continued to challenge conventional approaches. The new medium's unique structure also encouraged the team to reconsider its own processes of developing and producing campaigns. Zeederberg recalled his team moving away from the linear model of creating campaigns, where the account service department briefed the creative team, who conjured the campaign, which was then handed to the media department to insert into the media. It was replaced by what Zeederberg described as 'a collaborative, brainstorm, workshop-type approach'. This shift, he explained, stemmed from the realisation 'quite early on that you needed that mix of channel understanding, media understanding, creative messaging understanding, and planning, and customer insights'.[62] FCBi consequently redoubled its efforts to engage the media team – and with Hewitt's expertise and insights, they began to succeed.

Wilson-Brown's punt slowly began to pay off with FCBi-producing innovative campaigns that were unique and different. Its successful campaign for Nike football boots, which claimed that they offered unfair advantages over competitors, used a guerrilla viral-like approach. The campaign capitalised on digital media's 'wild West' status, where the conventional rules seemed to have gone out of the window. '[W]e actually at one point set up a website which was an anti-Nike protest. Playing on the whole Nike and child labour, and that sort of stuff', noted Zeederberg, adding 'how the hell we managed to get it through anybody, I don't know'.[63] While the press eventually exposed FCBi's tactics, its unorthodox approach nevertheless generated industry chatter and demonstrated that the internet was a fundamentally different medium to those that preceded it.[64] FCBi's pioneering work was duly noted by clients. Donovan recounted the growth of the operation, noting how they created 'about 40 websites in the space of about a year', which enabled them to win 'big, digital advertising accounts', including 'AOL which became, at that time, FCB's biggest revenue advertising client'.[65]

FCBi's growing success in the digital space coupled with the Dotcom Boom gave the impression that its future was well and truly on an upward trajectory. Zeederberg was therefore full of confidence when he met with his agency's managing director in mid-2001 to discuss FCBi's future:

> So, I clearly remember [laughs] going and having a meeting to sit down with Tim [Parker] at the Concrete Café, which is just outside

the offices, and I had brought all the financials, and all the plans, and where we were going, and how we had managed to break even in the first seven months when we thought that was only going to happen in the first two years. And where we were going next, and what there was all going to be, and had a whole long spiel for him. And we sat down, and I was about to launch into this, he goes, 'hang on, before you do anything, I have to tell you you're redundant'. [Laughs].[66]

Zeederberg was shocked at the time. Reflecting on it almost two decades later, he could see the broader external factors that caused FCBi's demise. Both were well outside of his control: the globalisation of the advertising industry and the collapse of the Dotcom Boom. Zeederberg thus explained that:

FCBi at the time was owned by Publicis, and then they got bought by True North. At a holding company level, FCB ... traded hands. And one of the first directions that came out of the acquisition was, "this internet thing is a complete waste of time and money, shut down FCBi."[67]

While FCBi 'had managed to break even in the first seven months when we thought that was only going to happen in the first two years' and the (expensive) new staff 'were paying their way', the operation's weak staff to revenue ratio saw the new regional director question the viability of FCBi.[68] And as the full impact of the Dotcom Crash became more apparent, FCBi's days were numbered. After 18 months, FCBi would be 'reabsorbed' back into FCB in October 2001 – the agency's press release found it more palatable to blame a 'soft online market' for FCBi's demise than to blame the structural or cultural problems at the agency.[69]

Looking back over the rise and fall of FCBi, Wilson-Brown was proud of what this initiative had achieved as well as his own role in it. He was, however, deeply disappointed by the actions of his superiors in the United States, which placed a greater emphasis on short-term profits ahead of long-term strategic leadership:

at the end of the day, they were just paying lip service ... it wasn't changing the culture of the worldwide network in any way at all ... the focus was on the numbers and we closed the department down.[70]

In light of FCBi's achievements and, indeed, the developments that subsequently occurred in the digital space, Wilson-Brown also mused on his own actions:

> I'm sorry in a way I didn't argue more strongly, because it was absolutely what we were doing was the right thing to be doing. Well, at that point we were ahead of the curve as well, you know, and they never caught up after that [Laughs].[71]

*** *** ***

At the beginning of the third decade of the twenty-first century, we have witnessed and now possess a fuller understanding of the profound disruption wrought by information technology and digital media since their emergence in the 1990s. Their impact has surpassed initial predictions, changing the face of advertising as well as the ways that the advertising industry conducts its business. This example of Schumpeter's creative destruction process, however, has overshadowed the lukewarm reception initially meted out to these technologies and the degree to which creative destruction can be an incremental process. As we have seen in this chapter, the absence of this story from the historical record not only illustrates oral history's capacity to capture and document such stories, but also reveals the challenges that business historians face when using other 'more conventional' sources – notably the trade press.

The trade press was alert to the arrival of the computer in the advertising industry and its potential impact on agencies. However, agencies were less excited than the trade press. The agencies' acquisition of computers proved a relatively slow but steady process. While ignorance and technophobia certainly affected the speed of this process, the primary concerns centred on the costs of such an investment. However, once the savings in terms of costs and time became apparent, agency managers were on board and staff had to follow. Email arrived in agencies with less fanfare. For the trade press, the new communication failed to spark any excitement. Born digital, it lacked the visual distinctiveness of the computer and its monitor. It was also difficult to see beyond the image of email as an updated memo system. And by the time everyone was using it, its newsworthiness had passed. Yet, interviewees were very aware of email's disruptive impact, both within the agency setting and with external stakeholders. The establishment of FCBi signalled a shift in the advertising industry's outlook on digital technology. Interviewees' discussion of its demise, however, revealed the degree to which the speed of progress in this space continued to be affected by entrenched cultural attitudes, agency hierarchies, and financial interests. The trade press scarcely covered FCBi's rise, while its fall was reduced to a brief statement drawn from an agency press release. Such coverage, it should be said, revealed more about the agency's own ambiguous attitude than any deliberate omission on the trade press' behalf.

The gaps between interviewee recollection and the reports in the trade press underscore the strengths of oral history on the one hand, and the weaknesses of using 'conventional' sources on the other. Our interviews with staff provided an opportunity to examine agency work at a more detailed level and to explore aspects that other sources might deem mundane, irrelevant, or simply unremarkable. Such insights are important in their own right, but they also create opportunities for business historians to consider the impact of broader contexts on business activities, operations, and structures. Reflections, observations, and comments in our interviews also challenged the narratives featured in the trade press, by revealing the degree to which ideas of newsworthiness inform what stories are highlighted, marginalised, or simply ignored. Business historians, who examine more recent periods where access to archival materials becomes more complicated, will inevitably be drawn to making greater use of more accessible trade press publications. While such publications remain essential and highly valuable sources, their perspective needs to be read critically – a task that oral history can help undertake. Thus, rather than singling out oral history for any 'academic health warning', it might be more prudent for business historians to apply this warning to all sources equally.

Notes

1 Haydon Bray, 'Sex and the Internet: Who's doing It', *AdNews*, 17 November 1995, 14.
2 Rob Oliver, 'Fear and Confusion in the Info Age', *Ad News*, 16 June 1995, 18.
3 Dominic Pearman, interview by Robert Crawford, 18 May 2020, Title No: 1654221, National Film & Sound Archive, ACT (hereafter NFSA).
4 Steven Toms and John Wilson, 'Business History: Agendas, Historiography and Debates', in *The Routledge Companion to Business History*, ed. John Wilson, Steven Toms, Abe de Jong and Emily Bucnea (Abingdon: Routledge, 2017), 10.
5 Kenton Wilkinson and Patrick Merle, 'The Merits of Challenges of using Business Press and Trade Journal Reports in Academic Research on Media Industries', *Communication, Culture & Critique* 6, no. 3 (2013): 416.

6 Robert Crawford, *Digital Dawn in Adland: Transforming Australian Agencies* (Abingdon, New York: Routledge, 2021).
7 John Sintras, interview by Robert Crawford, 25 May 2020, Title No: 1654635, NFSA.
8 *Ibid.*
9 John Bevins, interview by Robert Crawford, 10 May 2013, Title No: 1488437, NFSA.
10 Graham Nunn, interview by Robert Crawford, 21 May 2013, Title No: 1489208, NFSA.
11 Phil Hayden, interview by Robert Crawford, 10 July 2020, Title No: 1654246, NFSA.
12 Ian Robinson, 'Power to publish set to spread', Desktop Revolution Supplement, *Ad News*, 27 August 1993, 7.
13 Tony Hale, interview by Robert Crawford, 13 May 2020, Title No. 1654628, NFSA.
14 *Ibid.*
15 Paul McMillan, interview by Robert Crawford, 18 March 2019, Title No: 1653109, NFSA.
16 Sintras, interview.
17 Matt Donovan, interview by Robert Crawford, 29 May 2020, Title No: 1654231, NFSA.
18 Roger Rigby, interview by Robert Crawford, 2 May 2013, Title No: 1489295, NFSA.
19 Greg McIntyre, interview by Rosemary Francis, 9 September 2014, Title No: 1489187, NFSA.
20 Keith Aldrich, interview by Rosemary Francis, 15 June 2012, Title No: 1485200, NFSA.
21 *Ibid.*
22 Bevins, interview.
23 Justin Mansfield, 'The Desk top Revolution', *Ad News,* 31 May 1991, 21, 26; Tony Burrett, 'Big Agencies beef up Computer Power', Desktop Revolution Supplement, *Ad News*, 27 August 1993, 2.
24 John Cleen, 'PC Makers need "Common Touch" to boost Their Sales', *Marketing Week*, 13 November 1997, 32.
25 Tom Moult, interview by Robert Crawford, 11 May 2020, Title No: 1654630, NFSA.
26 Ed Brice and Peter Murphy, interview by Robert Crawford, 2 August 2019, Title No: 1653849, NFSA.
27 Kimberlee Wells, interview by Robert Crawford, 3 June 2019, Title No: 1653146, NFSA.
28 Paul McMillan, interview by Robert Crawford, 18 March 2019, Title No: 1653109, NFSA.
29 Tony Hale, interview by Robert Crawford, 13 May 2020, Title No: 1654628, NFSA.
30 Cummins, interview.
31 Sintras, interview.
32 Victor Maree, interview by Robert Crawford, July 23, 2019.
33 Cummins, interview.
34 Michael McEwen, interview by Robert Crawford, 28 November 2018, Title No: 1653841, NFSA.

35 Imogen Hewitt, interview by Robert Crawford, 1 June 2020, Title No: 1654235, NFSA.
36 *Ibid.*
37 Brice and Murphy, interview.
38 Cummins, interview.
39 Brice and Murphy, interview.
40 'MSN Hotmail, World's Largest E-Mail Provider, Surpasses 30 Million Member Milestone', PR Newswire, 1 December 1998; 'Hotmail hits a Million with free E-mail Service', *B&T Weekly*, 2 October 1998, 19.
41 Hale, interview.
42 *Ibid.*
43 Rob Oliver, 'Fear and Confusion in the Info Age', *Ad News*, 16 June 1995, 18.
44 Dave McCaughan, 'How to Advertise on the New Media', *Ad News*, 16 June 1995, 19. Pauline Hayes, 'Surfing the "Net for Profit"', *B&T*, 22 September 1995, 23. Allan Bonsall, 'To Net or not to Net?', *Ad News*, 3 May 1996, 29.
45 Laurence A. Canter, *How to Make a Fortune on the Information Superhighway: Everyone's Guerrilla Guide to Marketing on the Internet and Other On-line Services* (New York: Harper Collins, 1994); Michael Strangelove, *How to Advertise on the Internet: An Introduction to Internet-facilitated Marketing and Advertising* (Ottawa: Strangelove Internet Enterprises, 1994).
46 Sintras, interview.
47 Colin Wilson-Brown, interview by Robert Crawford, 6 May 2020, Title No: 1654341, NFSA.
48 *Ibid.*
49 *Ibid.*
50 Matt Donovan, interview by Robert Crawford, 29 May 2020, Title No: 1654231, NFSA.
51 *Ibid.*
52 *Ibid.*
53 *Ibid.*
54 Hewitt, interview.
55 *Ibid.*
56 Mike Zeederberg, interview by Robert Crawford, 13 May 2020, Title No: 1654626, NFSA.
57 Wilson-Brown, interview.
58 Zeederberg, interview.
59 Hewitt, interview.
60 *Ibid.*
61 Crawford, *Digital Dawn in Adland*, 36–37.
62 Zeederberg, interview.
63 *Ibid.*
64 Todd Lappin & Bruce Grierson, 'The Year in Ideas: A to Z; Corporate Jujitsu', *New York Times*, 9 December 2001, https://www.nytimes.com/2001/12/09/magazine/the-year-in-ideas-a-to-z-corporate-jujitsu.html, accessed 3 May 2022.
65 Donovan, interview.
66 Zeederberg, interview.

67 *Ibid*
68 *Ibid.*
69 Kris Ashton, 'Staff Shuffle as FCBi Closes', *AdNews*, 26 October 2001, https://www.adnews.com.au/yafNews/A24AB952-1DCD-460C-80C3E1479 ED47D82, accessed 3 May 2022.
70 Wilson-Brown, interview.
71 *Ibid.*

Conclusion

Continuing the Conversation

When Helen Bakewell commenced her career in consumer and economic research for Australian shopping centres in the early 1990s, she found herself in a pioneering position. As a result of the developments charted in Chapter 3, Lend Lease created a dedicated marketing position to gain deeper insights into consumer behaviour. As the sole, specialist retail analyst for the firm, Bakewell managed to build up an entire department that was drawing in millions of dollars. Her success was not lost on her competitors, who copied her approach and created their own in-house retail and shopping centre research departments. The sector's growing demand for such research would see Bakewell go on to create her own highly successful consultancy, Directional Insights. Outlining the retail industry's spectacular growth and development over the 1990s and the first decades of the 2000s, Bakewell discussed some of the differences between female and male consumers and its impact on the retail sector. Asked to comment on whether gender affected career progression in her own profession, Bakewell was clear: 'Yeah, look, it's always been really even. ... which is why I really like it. Gender has actually never been a barrier, I don't think. ... Yeah. By and large, I haven't seen that as an issue'.[1] As someone who had pioneered a new field offering essential insights into large businesses that were investing heavily in the retail market, it is perhaps unsurprising that Bakewell encountered few problems on account of gender – her competition was simply too small, while the market was too hungry for the insights her work was unearthing. However, when encouraged to consider the topic more broadly, notably the lack of women on the boards of major retail firms, Bakewell offered a more equivocal perspective:

> That's a different thing from day-to-day management of shopping centres. And that is a problem in Australia but that's not because

DOI: 10.4324/9781003171232-6

it's shopping centres or retailers, do you know what I mean? ... That's an Australian attitudinal problem, that's not a retail-based relationship. And I ... yeah that is quite frustrating. But, you know, having run my own business, if you want to get out and be a decision-maker and be a leader, there is opportunity to do that. And companies like Lend Lease and AMP, they probably lead the way on being family friendly, part-time, for men and women ...[2]

While gender had not been a key part of Bakewell's own narrative as a disrupter, oral history's capacity to unearth, engage, and probe demonstrated that it was not altogether absent from her story either. The opportunity to locate bigger themes and to unpack such complexities points to the challenges and the potential richness to be found in oral history testimony, but also underscores the critical need for a deeper understanding of oral history methods and methodology to make the most of them.

Bakewell's observations and comments, alongside those explored over the course of the four chapters of this book, help illustrate Rob Perks' pithy assertion that 'corporations are people too!'. Each person has a story to tell. Each has experiences, perspectives, and insights that matter. Their exclusion from the historical record has therefore been to the detriment of oral history and business history alike, creating gaps, biases, and generalisations. Our interviews with business leaders, managers, staff, and consumers help to put these actors and their stories back on to the historical record. However, applying oral history approaches to Schumpeter's concept of creative destruction does more than that. To this end, we believe that our interviews also help to reveal some of the internal mechanics and dynamics of this process and, indeed, to problematise them. In each chapter, we explored disruptions as well as attendant innovations stemming from them. Our interviewees collectively revealed that disruption and innovation did not necessarily occur suddenly, uniformly, or expansively. It was also experienced personally.

In Chapter 1, our exploration of supermarkets in the Australian context demonstrated that Coles' successful adaptation in the face of disruptive forces produced considerable internal instability as managers grappled with the scale and nature of change. Chapter 4 illustrates the way that disruptions and innovations wrought by the arrival of the digital age were largely downplayed or simply dismissed by advertising professionals, who were comfortable with the status quo. The dearth of oral history testimony does not completely account for the absence of such experiences on the historical record. As Chapters 2 and 3 reveal, mythmaking has also played an important role in concealing certain accounts and perspectives, while emphasising others. In exposing the emotions, values, and ideas that underpinned interviewee relationships with the Cadbury brand, the interviews with internal and external stakeholders in Chapter 2, demonstrated the importance of continuity amidst a sea of change. The myths perpetuated by various interviewees in Chapter 3 not only functioned to cast a positive and convincing account of the retail property industry and its contribution to communities, but also helped downplay the criticisms that had been levelled at it. Across the four chapters in the book, our interviewees' comments and reflections demonstrated that the process of creative destruction was only uniform in its variability. Creative destruction, as relayed through our interviews, might be more accurately viewed as a continual process (involving both transformation and reorganisation) rather than a revolution to be viewed in binary destruction–innovation terms.

Looking more broadly at oral history's contribution to business history, our chapters demonstrate the significance of intimacy. As individuals who hold a direct and often deep connection with business, businesses, and/or business practices, the interviewees possess the unique capacity to inform, enhance, challenge, correct, and animate the historical record – sometimes in the same breath. Intimate details and first-hand experiences provide access to business practices and business culture. They also enable business historians to reflect more broadly on the relationships between individuals, organisations, and their broader social, cultural, economic, and political contexts. In revealing both continuities and change, they provide an opportunity to identify the dynamics at play and to interrogate them more deeply.

The intimacy afforded by oral history provides an opportunity for business history to move beyond the image of the 'faceless' corporation and to reconsider the role of the individual. In prioritising the individual and foregrounding their experiences and insights, oral history interviews provide access to individual thoughts, motivations, and actions. They also allow business historians to consider how interviewees are affected, directly or indirectly, by a range of different factors and contexts. While the standard caveats apply to such accounts, they nevertheless expand the record and create new lines of enquiry.

The importance of oral history testimony is not restricted to what is actually stated or discussed in the interview. Oral history interviews can equally remind us why certain stories, experiences, or processes have gone undocumented by other sources. Business sensitivities, for example, are an abiding concern. Fears that competitors may access sensitive information mean that any such materials are closely guarded, and all too often destroyed. Intimate aspects of marketing practices or consumer reactions are thus lost in this way. The secret commissions and illegal activities noted in Chapter 3 were even more sensitive and were therefore never documented. Failed initiatives, such as FCBi, are similarly swept under the carpet. At the other end of the spectrum, other issues were not recorded on account of their mundanity. There were no records on the prior career histories of early shopping centre promotional marketers. Equally, there seemed little need to document the anxieties that staff experienced when composing their first emails, let alone maintain them for posterity. Costs similarly play a role in determining what is documented and what is not. If an initiative, action, or reaction is immaterial to the business' principal aims or goals, there is little impetus for spending time, effort, and, importantly, money on producing and maintaining such materials. As oral history is not necessarily constrained by these factors, it emerges as an integral, rather than supplementary resource for business historians.

Business historians can also benefit greatly from oral history's capacity to engage actively with sources. By speaking directly to business stakeholders, business historians are not only able to unearth new insights or details, they are also able to pursue issues and even challenge eye witness accounts. To this end, oral history can also play an important role in verifying other sources – a point vividly illustrated in Chapter 4. Such strengths should help ameliorate the cautionary concerns about oral history expressed by various business historians and demonstrate that oral history holds equal weight with other historical resources and approaches. Of course, we are not arguing that oral history is without its own issues, shortcomings, and challenges – far from it. But by engaging more deeply with the historiography in this space, we contend that business historians will be in a better position to capitalise on the strengths of oral history while continuing to address or limit its shortcomings.

While we have sought to put the case to business historians for using oral history, we argue that there is an equally compelling case for oral historians to pay much closer attention to business history and its capacity to enhance oral history as a field and a practice. In our introduction, we explored oral history's fractured relationship with business history and over the course of this book, we have sought to demonstrate how this relationship can be reconciled. Overcoming oral history's ambivalence towards business history requires us to consider the roots of this outlook. With its radical aim of giving voice to those who had traditionally been muted and/or excluded from the historical record, oral history's emphasis on 'history from below' has afforded little place for the privileged voice of business. Within this agenda, business history has been conflated with elite history. While elite stories are certainly integral to understanding business history, they only provide a partial account.[3] There are in fact many stakeholders, whose relationships with business are heterogenous and often complex. As our chapters demonstrate, the recollections and commentary shared by staff, middle-management, or consumers are as important and insightful as those recounted by leaders. While we have called for greater recognition of the diverse range of voices that business history can add to the record, it is worth recognising the contribution that interviews with business elites can make to oral history more generally. As Ylva Waldemarson observes, such interviews can paradoxically support oral history's radical agenda insofar as 'elite oral history like traditional oral history can compensate for the systematic lopsidedness of the written record'.[4] Interviews with individual leaders and managers, for example, can deliver richer, deeper, and more comprehensive insights than those documented in dry board meeting minutes or communiques forwarded to staff. The capacity of oral history interviews to produce commentary and reflection on events that were deliberately downplayed or even excluded from formal documentation, enhance our understanding of extant written and material archives.

Business history's embrace of oral history can also make a meaningful contribution to oral history work being undertaken in other historical fields. Interviews with staff and management, for example, can create connections with labour historians utilising oral history and, indeed, encourage more critical thinking about the fault lines between them. Oral history's capacity to open conversations between disparate fields or areas of focus creates scope for more holistic and nuanced perspectives of economic history, enabling it to contribute to broader historical debates, issues, or themes. Following on the accounting historian Theresa Hammond's call 'for more oral histories in order to achieve a basic understanding of the lived experience of LGBTQI+ people in the [accounting] industry', we contend that this call can be extended to the entire business sector.[5] Business history interviews can equally be used to establish new contexts for exploring issues pertaining to gender, class, ethnicity, and sexuality, and for generating further insights into them. By adopting a more inclusive view of business history that recognises its significance and relevance, as well as its capacity to generate new perspectives on broader historical themes and questions, oral history can welcome a lost relative back to the fold – and it will be better for it.

Notes

1 Helen Bakewell, interview by Matthew Bailey, 12 March 2015.
2 *Ibid.*
3 See also Geoffrey Jones & Rachael Comunale, 'Oral History and the Business History of Emerging Markets', *Enterprise & Society* 20, no. 1 (2019): 19–32; Valeria Giacomin, Geoffrey Jones and Erica H. Salvaj, 'Business Investment in Education in Emerging Markets since the 1960s', *Business History* 63, no. 7 (2021): 1113–43.
4 Ylva Waldemarson, 'Openness and Elite Oral History: The Case of Sweden', in *The Paradox of Openness: Transparency and Participation in Nordic Cultures of Consensus*, ed. Norbert Götz and Carl Marklund (Leiden, Boston, MA: Brill, 2015), 177.
5 Theresa Hammond, 'LGBTQ+ Accountants: A Call for Oral History Research', *Sustainability Accounting, Management and Policy Journal* 9, no. 5 (2018): 621.

Index

Note: Page numbers followed by "n" denote endnotes.

academic health warning 88, 106
Ad News 99
advertising industry 89, 105–6;
    internet growth 93–9; internet in
    trade press 99–105; sophistication
    of 89–93
Aldrich, Keith 92
American accounting systems 35
American retail case studies 25
Andrews, Gavin J. 35
anti-Nike protest 103
Apple Macintosh 90
Australia: advertising industry in
    89; creating community centres
    and retail town halls 79–81;
    grocery chains in 26; industry
    professionalisation 69–71; market
    research 71–4; retail property
    industry in 81; shopping centre
    development 68–9; shopping
    centre leases in 74; shopping
    centres in 67; supermarkets in 111;
    understanding customer 75–8

Bakewell, Helen 110, 111
Balmer, John 46
Berg, Hazel de 1, 17n1
Best, Ted 50, 51
Bevins, John 90, 93
Black, Carol 56
Black, Susan 56
Bloom, Robert 12
Boyce, Harry 39

Bradbury, Bevan 29–30, 32, 33
Bray, Haydon 87, 88
Brice, Ed 94
Briggs, Alan 71, 72
British oral history 9
Brockbank, Louise 100
Brown, Derreck 51, 52
Brown, Robert 55, 60
Burnett, Leo 89, 95
business change, social and cultural
    dimensions of 5
business cultures 12, 112
business decision-making processes 9
business historians 45, 106, 113
business history: Cadbury brand 45;
    and disruption 3–6; embrace of
    oral history 114; interviews 114;
    journals, use of oral history in 9;
    and oral history 7–8
business sensitivities 112–13

Cadbury 45–7; business history
    45; collective experience 54–61;
    consumer relationships with 57, 58;
    establishing presence 47–8; growth
    in Australia 48; in-store presence
    and packaging strategies 59;
    internal and external stakeholders
    interviews 62; interviewee
    relationships with 112; long-term
    commitment to marketing 58;
    narratives of 45; staff loyalty 49–54
Cadbury, John 47

capitalism 6
'the capitalist engine' 4
Chinoy, Ely 36
Chubb, Greg 75, 80
Clapham, J. H. 9
Clarke, Caroline A. 30
Clarke, Richard 66, 67, 69–71, 73
Clemenger BBDO, Sydney 92
Cohen, Lizabeth 80
Coles 24–6, 39–40, 111; family life
    of managers 35–9; importing
    supermarkets 26–8; 'Nobody
    Knows Quite What is Best to
    Do' 32–5; organisational shadow
    structure 29–32
Coles, Edgar 26, 33
Coles, Robert 27, 33, 34
Coles, Wilf 37
Collins, Marilyn 12
communication: digital and analogue
    modes of 94; internal 94, 95;
    traditional broadcast model of 98
community centres 79–81
computers 90–1, 93, 94, 105
Comunale, Rachael 13
consumer: relationships with
    Cadbury 57, 58; understanding
    75–8
consumption expenditure 78
continents 25
convenience-oriented neighbourhood
    centres 68
conventional business history 13
corporate branding 46
'Corporate Voices: Institutional and
    Organisational Oral Histories' 7
corporate-wife-as-victim analyses 38
'Corporations are People Too'
    (Perks) 7
Crawford, Robert 12
creative destruction 4, 15, 46, 67, 89,
    105, 111
Cummins, Sean 95, 97
customer-centric marketing theory 55
customer relationship marketing
    (CRM) 102

Dallimore, Roy 26
Davies, Andrea 12
deep market research 75
de-industrialisation 6

Dickens, S. E. 28, 34
digital advertising 102–3
Dimasi, Tony 74, 75
Dine, Pauline 61
direct marketing agency 101
discount department stores (DDSs)
    68, 77
disruption: business history and 3–6;
    transformed retailing 67
disruptive innovation 4, 26, 29
Donovan, Matt 91, 100, 101
Dotcom Boom 99, 103, 104
Dotcom Crash 104
Dru, Jean-Marie 5
Durepos, Gabrielle 14

economic growth 6
The Economist 3
Edwards, Dorothy 60
Edwards, Thomas Elford 48
Elphick, Graham 55, 59
email 93–5, 98, 105
external stakeholders 62, 95

FCBi 100–6, 113
food retailing 29
Fookes, Mark 72
Foote, Cone & Belding (FCB) 91,
    99–104
Fridenson, Patrick 14
Frisch, Ragnar 5

gender 110, 111
Giacomin, Valeria 13
Goffee, Rob 36
Gordon, Wendy 55
Gransbury, Lucy 45, 59–60
Grdosic, Sonja 54, 57
Great Depression 26
*The Great Disruption: How Business
    is Coping with Turbulent Times*
    (Wooldridge) 3
great man approach 9
Greyser, Stephen 46
grocery chains 27
Gruen, Victor 79–80
Guild, David 32

Hale, Tony 90, 91, 94, 98
Hammond, Theresa 12
Harvey, David 6

Hayden, Phil 90–1
Heath, Rod 53
heritage marketing 46
heritage marketing scholarship 46
Hewitt, Imogen 96, 97, 102
historical training 8
History of the French Revolution 8
Holland, Peter 80
Hornery, Stuart 73
hotmail 98
Hyland, Barry 49, 50, 53
Hynes, Brian 80

identity 11, 14
industry professionalisation 69–71, 74
innovation 3–4
'Innovation and the Evolution of
    Industries' (Malerba) 6
Integrated Services Digital Network
    (ISDN) 96
internal communication 94, 95
internal organisational disruption
    27–8
internal stakeholders 62
ISDN *see* Integrated Services Digital
    Network (ISDN)
Ives, Rocelyn 61

Jebb, Reg 72
Joel, Asher 1, 2, 17n1
Jones, Geoffrey 13

Kanter, Rosabeth Moss 15, 29, 31, 38
Keulen, Sjoerd 13
Kroeze, Ronald 13, 14
Kroger Grocery & Baking
    Company 33

Lend Lease 66, 70, 73, 74, 110;
    marketing evolution 71
Lloyd, Michael 66, 67, 71–3, 76, 79
long-term strategic leadership 104
Lonie, Michael 72, 80
Loveless, Doug 51, 52
Lowy, Frank 70

MacRobertson 51, 58
Malerba, Franco: 'Innovation and
    the Evolution of Industries' 6
*Management & Organizational
    History* 13

managerial career 37
managers, family life of 35–9
Maree, Victor 95
marketing: evolution of 71;
    promotion-oriented 72;
    promotions-based 81
marketing historians 12
marketing industry 46
Marketing Week 93
market research 71–4
mass internal migration 68
May, Andrew 80
Mayhew, Henry 8
McEwen, Michael 96
McIntyre, Greg 92
McKenzie, Jim 32–5
McKinlay, Alan 14
McMillan, Paul 91, 94
memory 11
Merle, Patrick 88
Michelet, Jules 8
Miller, Frank 51
Mitchell, Ronald 12, 13
Moult, Tom 93–4
multi-layered shopping centre
    model 76
'mum-and-dad' retailers 69, 70
Murphy, Peter 97–8
Musacchio Adorisio, Anna Linda 13
Mutch, Alistair 13
Myer 73, 77–9

narratives, of Cadbury 45
National Director of Leasing 70
National Library of Australia
    (NLA) 1
Nevins, Allan 8–9; great man
    approach 9
Newton, Ian 69–71
'Nobody Knows Quite What is Best
    to Do' 32–5
North, Thomas 24–6
Nunn, Graham 90

OHA *see* Oral History Association
    (OHA)
Oliver, Rob 87, 88, 99
O'Neil, Dave 57, 59
oral historians 10, 14, 113
oral history: business history and 7–8;
    in business history journals, use of

9; development of 7; interviews 2, 112; limitations and weaknesses of 11; recalibrating 11–14; with retail property 67; testimony 112; value of 82
oral history archive 25
Oral History Association (OHA) 10
Oral History Society annual conference 7
organisational culture 9, 15, 25
organisational politics 29, 30
organisational shadow structure 29–32
organizational men 37

Parker, Lee 11
Patterson, George 91, 94
Pearman, Dominic 87, 88
Perks, Rob 111; 'Corporations are People Too' 7
personal memories 56
pre-planned shopping centres 68
primitive supermarkets 25
professionalisation 81; industry 69–71, 74
promotion-oriented marketing 72
promotions-based marketing 81
public relations 1–2

QuarkXPress 92
Queensland Penney's 30

Ranke, Leopold von 8
Rashleigh, Mark 49, 50
Remington, John 51
retailers 68–70; databases 74; 'mum-and-dad' 69, 70; specialty 69
retail mix 74–7
retail property 67
retail property industry 67, 68, 81, 112
retail property market research career 72
retail stores, price standardisation on 35
retail town halls 79–81
retail trading hours, deregulation of 78
Rigby, Roger 92
Robinson, Lance 27, 28

Rogers, Everett M. 5
Rosaldo, Renato 67
Routledge Companion to Business History (Toms and Wilson) 88
Rushbrook, Carole 52, 57, 61
Ruthven, Elizabeth 56, 59

Sainsbury, Charlotte 50, 52, 53
Salvaj, Erica H. 13
Samuelson Talbot & Partners 94
Sandercock, Leonie 80
Saunders, John 72
Scase, Richard 36
Schroder, John 78
Schumpeter, Joseph 3–5, 24, 25, 46, 62, 111
Schwarzkopf, Stefan 54
Scott, Andrew 79
Seabrook, Graeme 35
Second World War 1–2, 8, 25, 26, 36, 48
self-service 25, 27
Shopes, Linda 14
shopping centres 68, 69; advertising and architecture in 77; as community spaces 80; proliferation and growing scale of 73; retail mix of 75
Sikka, Prem 12
Sintras, John 89, 91, 95, 99
Sliwa, Martyna 13
Smart, Trevor 58
Smith, Penelope 49
spans markets 25
Spearritt, Peter 81
specialty retailers 69
staff loyalty, Cadbury 49–54
stakeholders 46; external 95; internal and external 62
Stanfield, Betty 49
Stanford, Tim 53
State Library of Victoria, Melbourne 25
stock-taking systems 33
Stubbs, David 57
Summers, Margaret 57, 58
supermarket disruption 36
supermarkets 24–5, 29, 39–40; in Australia 111; growth of

36; importing 26–8; internal
organisational disruption 27–8

Taylor, Gwen 52
Taylor, Scott 14
Tedman, Dennis 56, 57
Terry, Graham 78
Thiessen, Janis 14, 25
Thomas, Jim 28
Thompson, F. L. 27
Thompson, Paul: *The Voice of the
Past* 7
'three Ds' 99
'Tomorrow's Newspaper' 27
Toms, Steven: *Routledge Companion
to Business History* 88
Trade Practices Act 35
trade press 105, 106; internet in
99–105

Urde, Mats 46

Vervloet, Jasmijn 14
The Voice of the Past (Thompson) 7

Waldemarson, Ylva 114
Walton, John 14
Wells, Kent 52
Wells, Kimberlee 94
Westfield 70, 71–2
Whyte, William H. 80
Wilkinson, Kenton 88
Wilson-Brown, Colin 99, 100, 102–5
Wilson, John: *Routledge Companion
to Business History* 88
Wooldridge, Adrian: *The Great
Disruption: How Business is Coping
with Turbulent Times* 3
work life balance 26
work-life experience 9

Zeederberg, Mike 100–4
Zundel, Mike 67